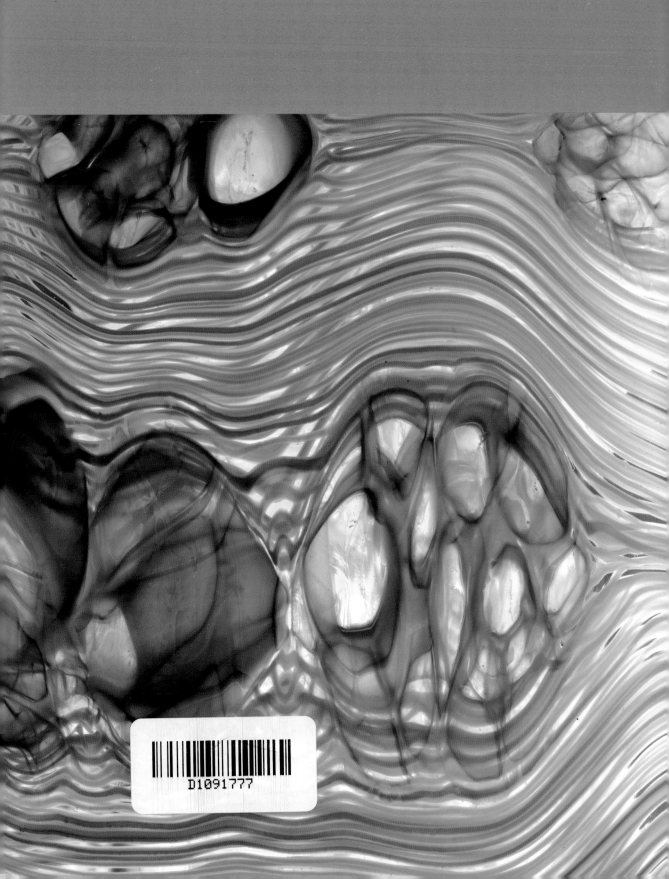

Viva Vetro! Glass Alive!

VENICE AND AMERICA

Essays
Susanne K. Frantz
Matthew Kangas

Exhibition Curator
Sarah Nichols

Carnegie Museum of Art

Viva Vetro! Glass Alive! VENICE AND AMERICA

Published in conjunction with the exhibition
Viva Vetro! Glass Alive! Venice and America
Carnegie Museum of Art, May 12–September 16, 2007
organized by Sarah Nichols.

The exhibition is supported by "Pittsburgh Celebrates Glass," made possible by the generosity of many foundations and corporations, including the Richard King Mellon Foundation, The Heinz Endowments, the Claude Worthington Benedum Foundation, PNC Financial Services, and Highmark.

Additional support is provided by the Henry L. Hillman Fund, The Fellows of Carnegie Museum of Art, and the National Endowment for the Arts.

The exhibition catalogue was made possible by The Beal Publication Fund and the Henry Lea Hillman, Jr. Foundation.

CARNEGIE
MUSEUM
OF ART

Carnegie Museum of Art
4400 Forbes Avenue
Pittsburgh, PA 15213–4080
www.cmoa.org

Viva Vetro! Glass Alive! Venice and America

ISBN 978-0-88039-048-4

© 2007 Carnegie Museum of Art, Carnegie Institute

"Venice and America: Cultural Exchanges in Glass"
"A Conversation with Lino Tagliapietra"
"A Conversation with Benjamin Moore"
© 2007 Matthew Kangas

"The Italian Connection: Americans at Venini"
© 2007 Susanne K. Frantz

COVER: Dorothy Hafner, American, b. 1952; with Lino Tagliapietra, maestro, Italian, b. 1934; *Aurora*, 1995, glass, blown and fused, with *tesserae*; The Corning Museum of Glass, Corning, New York

INSIDE FRONT COVER: Kait Rhoads, American, b. 1968; *Fashion Plate* (detail), 2005, glass, blown, with cane and *murrine*; Carnegie Museum of Art

TITLE PAGE: Charles Lin Tissot, designer, American, 1904–1994; Venini & C., manufacturer, Italian, 1929–1985; *Chess Set* (detail), 1955, glass, blown and hot-worked, with *zanfirico*; Lent by Charles Luke

PAGE 6: Alfredo Barbini, Italian, b. 1912; *Biennale Vase* (detail), 1962, glass, hot-worked, with *sommerso* and *battuto*; The Museum of Modern Art, New York

PITTSBURGH
CELEBRATES
GLASS
2007

Contents

Foreword

MORE THAN 200 YEARS AGO, A SMALL GLASS factory opened in Pittsburgh, and the city's history with glass began. Since then, glass production in Pittsburgh has included everything from tableware to architectural materials to flat-screen televisions manufactured by industrial powerhouses. Carnegie Museum of Art, founded in 1895, acquired soon thereafter its first historical glass object—a humble and extremely functional plate. In the following century, its glass collection has grown to more than 1,300 objects dating from ancient Roman times to the present.

Glass has outlived its sister industries, iron, coal, and steel, and today continues to be a vital component of the regional economy as well as a source of local pride. Not coincidentally, it has become a focus of the museum's collecting and exhibition programs, the emphasis gradually shifting from glass as a material for industrial design to glass as a medium for artists.

Acquired in 1984, *Cylinder* by Dale Chihuly can rightly be seen as a founding object for the museum's collection of contemporary Venetian and American glass. The collection received an important boost from Maxine and William Block's generous gifts of 76 glass objects, principally between 2002 and 2007, including significant works by artists featured in this exhibition.

This year marks the sixth anniversary of the Pittsburgh Glass Center, a studio, gallery, teaching, and production facility dedicated to supporting and highlighting artists working in glass. Also in 2007, "Pittsburgh Celebrates Glass" is presenting a citywide, yearlong program of exhibitions, artists' installations, symposia, performances, conferences, and events dedicated to the beauty, traditions, and cultural vitality of glass. Highlights of the year include the *Chihuly at Phipps: Gardens and Glass* installation at Phipps Conservatory and Botanical Gardens. We are delighted to participate in this landmark celebration through the exhibition *Viva Vetro! Glass Alive! Venice and America.*

It has long been recognized that the seeds of the American studio glass movement can be traced in part to several historic encounters, beginning in the 1950s, between some adventurous American artists and designers and a few open-minded and generous-spirited Italian glassmakers. American scholarship has stressed the impact of these encounters on American craft and contemporary art: a huge increase in technical sophistication, a shift from individual to team and workshop methods of production, a greater appreciation for color, and the rise of glass from a minor craft to a major art form in a relatively brief time. The emphasis has been on distinctively American achievements and the continual redrawing of boundaries between traditional craft and contemporary art to accommodate new and often dazzling evidence of creativity.

As its dual-language title implies, this exhibition suggests that other perspectives may be brought to bear on so compelling a story. In particular, the question of the impact of the Americans on Italian glassmakers has rarely been considered. Indeed, the Murano factories have incorporated little of the work of their American protégés in their own production lines, and they continue to favor traditional methods and designs even today. As a result, it is easy to conclude that only the Americans found this exchange to be a transformative experience. However, as this exhibition demonstrates, some Italian master glassmakers, encouraged by their exposure to American artists in Venice, ventured out of the Murano factories to the United States and have established careers as independent creative artists on the American model.

The essayists for this catalogue provide complementary histories of the Americans' experiences and learnings from Venice. Susanne Frantz, drawing on primary research and interviews with many of the artists involved, stresses the importance of individual initiative, personal relationships, and shared passion for the unique qualities of glass as a material for creativity. Matthew Kangas examines the critical impact of converging social, political, and economic forces in post–World War II Italy on the glassmaking industry.

He considers the reasons why traditionally reticent Italian manufacturers suddenly opened their doors to strangers and the way labor unrest and the erosion of the glassblowing hierarchy within Venetian factories provided opportunities for Americans to learn from the Italian masters. The complexity of the actual experiences of Italian masters and American students comes through in the two interviews that follow the essays.

Together, these stories relate the history of contemporary American glass to some of the classic debates of art history, such as the eternal tension between artistic inventiveness and craft discipline as well as the relative importance of social and historical factors as catalysts for artistic innovation and cultural change.

As the historical perspective on this subject lengthens, more questions will undoubtedly emerge even as others are resolved. Among the fields of contemporary craft, art, and design, directions change and new methods, new artists, new controversies, and new insights will continue to confound and delight us.

RICHARD ARMSTRONG
The Henry J. Heinz II Director

Director's Acknowledgments

We are deeply indebted to the funders of "Pittsburgh Celebrates Glass," the Richard King Mellon Foundation, in particular, for its sustained interest in Pittsburgh's ongoing evolution as one of the country's premiere arts destinations. As always, The Fellows of Carnegie Museum of Art provided important and timely help in the organization of the exhibition. Its catalogue has been underwritten in part by the Henry Lea Hillman, Jr. Foundation. We gratefully acknowledge the further assistance of the National Endowment for the Arts.

Sarah Nichols, former curator of decorative arts and more recently adjunct curator, has overseen this exhibition from its inception with the rigor and insight that have distinguished her long career. She was ably assisted by Rachel Delphia, assistant curator of decorative arts, and Lucy Stewart, assistant curator of education.

We cite with pleasure the exceptionally handsome presentation of the show as planned by Anne Mundell, likewise its memorable graphic identity and this catalogue designed by Dale McNutt. The museum's staff is to be commended also for its collegiality, attention to detail, and high standards.

(fig. 1) Aerial View of Murano.

Venice and America: Cultural Exchanges in Glass

MATTHEW KANGAS

Introduction: Cultural Interchange

There have been a number of cultural interchanges between Europe and the United States since the end of World War II that have shaped the direction of postwar art. Some notable examples include the impact of Abstract Expressionism on French, Italian, and Scandinavian artists (even if that impact was fraught with controversy over the direct and indirect levels of sponsorship interventions from governmental entities such as the Central Intelligence Agency[1]); the development of Pop art by British artists, including Richard Hamilton, who anticipated the style before their more famous American counterparts, including Andy Warhol and Roy Lichtenstein (a fact that English art critic Lawrence Alloway, who coined the term Pop, repeatedly reminded American audiences[2]); the dominance, in the 1980s, of Neo-Expressionist work first by German painters Georg Baselitz and Sigmar Polke and then by Americans Julian Schnabel and David Salle, who drew inspiration from early 20th-century German Expressionism; and, in Italy, the conception of Arte

Povera by artists such as Mario Merz and the Greek transplant Iannis Kounellis, whose low-profile, casually placed installations garnered a small but enthusiastic American following.

A similar symbiosis in art glass began early in the cold war years, when artisans, artists, and designers in Italy's handmade glass center, Murano Island in the Venice Lagoon, were caught off-guard as American artists, including Harvey Littleton, Thomas Stearns, and Robert Willson, began showing up to learn about glassmaking and, in some cases, to make glass on their own. *Viva Vetro! Glass Alive! Venice and America* focuses on the final half of the 20th century, a period that saw unprecedented economic growth and artistic innovation in both Italy and the United States. The complex exchanges between artists from these two countries working in glass constitute one of the richest developments in American craft during the last 50 years.

That said, some would argue that the comparable relationship between American ceramics and Japanese clay

art was a bigger and broader phenomenon.[3] However, the link between U.S. and Italian glassmakers continues to this day, whereas the mutual influence of Japanese and American ceramic artists seems to have peaked at the end of the last century, especially following the deaths of two major proponents, Peter Voulkos, in 2002, and Ken Ferguson, in 2005. Without diminishing the achievements of and the numerous exchanges between Japanese ceramic artists coming to the United States (for example, Ryoji Koie, Kimpei Nakamura, and Mutsuo Yanagihara) and U.S. clay artists going to Japan (among them, Rick Hirsch, Gary Moler, and Robert Sperry), the relations between the Americans and Italians started earlier, went on longer, and were more sustained in terms of having a proliferating impact within all of American glass art.

With the exception of Masami Koda and Akio Takamori, few Japanese artists moved to the United States permanently or made extended, repeated sojourns. Among the Italian glass artists, however, the cross-continental forays of Francesco "Checco" Ongaro, Loredano Rosin,

Giuseppe "Pino" Signoretto, and Lino Tagliapietra had tremendous ramifications for American artists working in glass; the influence of the visiting Italians served to raise skill levels, to promote the value of teamwork, and to create historical models à la façon de Venise, with its frilly, complicated, and elegant style.

Conversely, the 37 summers spent in Venice by Willson between 1957 and 1996, along with protracted stays by, among others, Tina Aufiero, James Carpenter, Dale Chihuly, Dan Dailey, Marvin Lipofsky, Richard Marquis, Benjamin Moore, Ginny Ruffner, Stearns, and Toots Zynsky, had greater influence on the Venetians than has been previously acknowledged.[4] Freedom of expression, above all, was the creative paradigm the Americans offered, not so different from the example provided by the Abstract Expressionists, whose works were exhibited at the various Venice Biennales during those early years.

When the American artists started to arrive in Venice after World War II, they were in search of both inspiration and information. Until the discovery in 1962, in Toledo, Ohio, of lower melting temperatures for glass, there was little possibility that glass art could be made outside of a factory setting. A few years before that pivotal technological breakthrough, the trickle of American artists to Italy had begun in earnest.

Italian Glass Before the Americans

Venetian glass has always been global, its influence always a two-way street. With Venice's domination of maritime trade along the Mediterranean seaboard in the 16th and 17th centuries, examples of Byzantine, Chinese, Persian, and Egyptian glass all came to the Serene Republic. Indeed, as Jutta Page has pointed out, when the original imports wore out or were broken, and as the Venetians noted a growing European market for exotic "foreign" styles of glass, emulations, copies, and outright fraudulent examples were promptly created.[5] For example, not knowing how to read Arabic calligraphy decoration on Byzantine goblets, Venetian enamellists created phony Arabic calligraphy that acted purely as ornament. The point is that, despite their own draconian measures to protect Venetian trade secrets, Venetian glassmakers were always open to borrowing and stealing from other cultures' styles and techniques.

Recent scholarship by both Italian and American art historians has filled in gaps and finally given American artists proper acknowledgment for their role in the history of Venetian glass.[6] The socioeconomic situation in Italy after World War II was dire at first. As chronicled in films by Vittorio De Sica (The Bicycle Thief, 1948) and Roberto Rossellini (Rome—Open City, 1945), poverty, crime, and shortages were widespread. By 1955, however, Italian architects and designers were stepping in to creatively refurbish the Murano glasshouses, whose output had fallen below prewar numbers due to the

disappearance of tourism and the unavailability of imported raw materials.

The cold war period was a fascinating time to arrive in Italy. The country's position within the American sphere of influence was secure. Although a Communist government was nearly elected on several occasions, the Christian Democratic Party rose to power in 1943 and continued its influence for the next 50 years. The loss of Italy's colonies in Africa was offset by rapid postwar modernization of industry, fueled in large part by cheap labor in and from the south (see Luchino Visconti's 1960 film Rocco and His Brothers) and the discovery of natural gas in the Po River valley in the north, crucially near Venice. The need to generate export income and taxes was great because the country was saddled with massive war reparations.

The Communists were shut out of Italy's coalition governments thanks to pressure from the Vatican and the U.S. emissary Clare Booth Luce. In return for this compromise of national sovereignty, the Italians received, in addition to the Marshall Plan (which ended in 1952), a $1 billion loan in 1964, following a package of other loans, grants, and gifts aimed at alleviating the enormous war debt.[7]

Artistically, by 1950, despite the bright hopes of architect Carlo Scarpa working for the renowned glasshouse Venini & C., as well as designers from before the war who were gearing back up, including Ercole Barovier and

Napoleone Martinuzzi,[8] the bulk of Venetian glass was still a sad mixture of filigree beakers and kitschy figurines, what critic William Warmus has called "dragon-tail goblets in garish colors,"[9] made chiefly for German tourists who were, ironically, the first Europeans to return to Italy after the ignominious defeat of both countries.

What Rosa Barovier Mentasti has called the "Rationalist inspiration that would prevail in Italy" after World War II was the result of the continuation of Scarpa's influence at Venini.[10] However, Scarpa's efforts did little to raise the general level of quality throughout the rest of Murano. A few other Venetians, including Alfredo Barbini, Mario Pinzoni, Flavio Poli, and Archimede Seguso, also held to a new formal rigor shorn of fussy adornment. In addition, glasshouse owners and directors such as Paolo Venini at Venini & C. and Ermanno Toso at Fratelli Toso encouraged what Mentasti describes as the new "20th-century look"; yet the 20th century was already half over by the time Murano got around to catching up with it. To be fair, the long Fascist interregnum (1922-1945) had led to streamlined styles, thanks in most part to Dino Martens and Martinuzzi, among others, but the products of this era were swept under the car-pet out of embarrassment because of their attachment to a maligned politics. (As we shall see, the modern, machinelike forms and appurtenances of this style would be revived in 1988 by Chihuly, who came upon a private collection of Mussolini-era glass while on his honeymoon in Venice in 1987.)

Italian glass in 1950 was at a crossroads. It was still licking its wounds after the war, temporarily cut off from the first modernizing influences of the Fascist era, and unable as yet to move forward to regain its prior international acclaim or to achieve full economic recovery through international trade expositions, rebuilt export markets, and the approval of wealthy Western European collectors and Milanese cognoscenti. Would Italian glass ever reclaim its former prestige, which reached its pinnacle in the 16th and 17th centuries? The answer lay in increased foreign input—in terms of both imported ideas and the growing revival of a once vigorous export market west of the Lagoon.

American Glass Before the Italians

The United States, with its first glass factories in New Jersey, West Virginia, Ohio, and upstate New York, did not develop the strong artistic styles that were desired abroad until the mid to late 19th century, when Louis Comfort Tiffany took out three patents on stained glass, mosaic tile, and metallic oxide techniques; these inventions were considered so groundbreaking that they became the focus of industrial espionage visits to New York sponsored by the French government.[11] What Tiffany did with his innovations was ultimately more important than how he discovered them.

American glass was primarily factory-based (Corning, Pilgrim, Fenton, and Libbey-Owens-Ford) until 1962, when Dominick Labino discovered a new glass formula using lower melting temperatures and worked with

Littleton to present a series of workshops and seminars at the Toledo Museum of Art, which were attended by prominent ceramic artists teaching in university settings. Because of the lower melting temperatures, studio-based rather than factory-based artists could work more independently and experimentally, and therefore Littleton and Labino called the breakthrough the birth of American studio glass. This was a serious misnomer, and remains one to this day. The home studio was too small a setting to accommodate the teams that were necessary for ambitious glassmaking; on the other hand, those same teams were too small to be accommodated by the large American factories. The setting for post-Toledo glassmaking was a fusion that was closer to the model of the Italian factory, or *fabbrica*, which was more like a big studio than an American factory. Chihuly's "Boathouse" studio/factory on Lake Union in Seattle became the new paradigm for American glassmaking.

Littleton would pursue the model of the one-man, one-blowpipe studio for many years. This may have been an extreme reaction to his own childhood, which was spent at the Corning Glass Works, where his father was director of research. But rather than representing what he thought would be the new alternative to American factory settings, Littleton's studio practice became the exception. In fact, the term "studio glass" is neither fully accurate nor appropriate. All of the Americans and Italians who worked together on Murano did so in small- or medium-size production sites. Most worked in either big studios (such as Barbini's) or very small factories (such as Venini and Fratelli Toso). More than one person—in some instances up to ten—were always involved. Littleton's obsolete model was too indebted to his own background in American studio pottery, which indeed could involve only one man and one throwing wheel in a studio at home. For glass, such a setting was not conducive to ambitious and important work.

Littleton's 1942 *Female Torso* is widely considered to mark the beginning of American studio glass, but this, too, was made at the Corning factory, while the artist was there on a summer internship. Earlier American artists such as Edris Eckhardt and Michael and Frances Higgins were making glass in small kilns at home, but often with great difficulty. The apex of American glass art during the pre-Toledo period was the work designed by Frederick Carder in the Steuben factory at Corning (Carder's Steuben Glass Works became part of the Houghton family's Corning Glass Works in 1918; the division was reorganized as Steuben Glass in 1933).

Marc Chagall, John Steuart Curry, Salvador Dalí, and Sidney Waugh, among other renowned artists, designed crystal plates in the 1930s and 1940s that were executed as limited-production lines at Steuben. Still, the desire to make more adventurous glass sculptures persisted and was not assuaged, really, until after the next generation of Americans such as Stearns, Willson,

and Charles Lin Tissot visited, observed, and worked in Venice and then returned to the United States to adapt their newly acquired bodies of knowledge: in Willson's case, he immediately made plans to return to Murano the following summer. It was the Americans' impetus toward the sculptural that would push the Muranese masters and technicians into an area generally regarded as infeasible and less lucrative than the endless variety of fancy tourist glassware.

During the decades of the Italian hosts, grumbling about, poking fun at, and overcharging the visiting Americans, Venetian glass was rescued and restored, once again refreshed by foreign intervention and transformed into an international cultural product of high repute. Glassblowing was pushed to new heights of radical experimentation. Solid glass sculpture made on the pipe, called *massiccio*, became a Venetian standard, thanks to the hefty push by the Americans, who kept coming back each summer.

Americans in Italy

Venezia

Da una barca
Venezia è là dove
Le case crescono dall'acqua
Le gente camminano sulle onde
Tutte le fanciulle,
Chi sono talmente arrotondate.
Non può essere vero.
—Robert Willson[12]

The magic of Venice—its beauty and infinite possibilities —attracted a diverse roster of American glass artists, including Eugene Berman, Claire Falkenstein, Kenneth George Scott, Stearns, Tissot, and Willson. All made journeys to the city in the early 1950s, interested in the expertise and facilities available there for making glass objects, from tableware and vessels to sculptures. As exhibitions such as *Italian Glass 1930-1970: Masterpieces of Design from Murano and Milan* have demonstrated, Italy's prewar achievements were better known to American audiences than the accomplishments made during the slower recovery of the postwar years. The design of high-end tableware and *objets d'art* rather than unique sculptures or elaborate presentation pieces predominated. However, as Susanne Frantz points out in her essay in this publication, one factory stood out in its openness and willingness to entertain and even hire foreigners: Venini & C. The owner, Paolo Venini, who inherited an older firm named Vetri Soffiati Muranesi Cappellin Venini & C., knew that, to become competitive in the international glass export market, modernity rather than historicism had to be achieved, assimilated, and then surpassed. The Venini products, eventually sold at such high-end American department stores as Kaufmann's, Neiman-Marcus, and Bloomingdale's, followed designs by prominent Italian architects such as Scarpa. Simple, often solid-color forms stood in high relief to the "dragon-tail goblets in garish colors" that constituted the bulk of Murano output at the time and even to this day.

Scott and Berman worked at Venini as early as 1950–1951, followed by Tissot in 1955 and Stearns, Venini's first Fulbright scholar, in 1960-1962. The last worked with maestro Arturo "Boboli" Biasutto and was also the first of the Americans to work with Ongaro, the man who would eventually break them all in. Stearns' long series of blown forms resembles, among other things, a doge's hat. Tall forms with colored *incalmo* sections suggest the water reflections in Venice's Grand Canal and the Lagoon. In these works, the color lies beneath the clear *incalmo* layer. Stearns was named resident guest designer in 1961, and several of his designs went into production. Dubbed "Tomaso Sternini'" or "Sternini de Venini'" by hot-shop floor workers, Stearns was among the most successful of the Americans who worked there in the 1950s.

With Paolo Venini's death in 1959, his son-in-law Ludovico Diaz de Santillana became the firm's new director. An educator by training, de Santillana was even more open to experimental work than his predecessor. Before discussing his successful reign at Venini and his camaraderie with visiting American artists, however, it

(**fig. 2**) Robert Willson and Licio Zuffi smoothing glass sculpture with Marcello Costantini, at Fratelli Toso Factory, Venice, 1968.

(**fig. 3**) Alfredo Barbini's factory and garden, Murano Island, Venice, July 1976.

is necessary to examine the most important American in Venice outside of Venini.

Willson, like Littleton (who was in Venice briefly in 1955), was a ceramic sculptor and university professor who saw his own work as better suited to *massiccio*, the solid-glass sculptural technique usually begun by massing glass on the blowpipe and often finished in a mold. Having spent his youth in Mexico exploring Mayan ruins, painting frescoes with Diego Rivera, and socializing with Rivera, Frida Kahlo (whom he photographed), and Leon Trotsky, Willson was fully comfortable in the role of handsome, glamorous outsider in a foreign country.

Arriving in Venice in 1956, on a travel grant made possible by Carder at Corning, Willson returned the following summer to work at the Toso brothers' family firm, Fratelli Toso (founded in 1854). Licio Zuffi was the first maestro to execute Willson's designs at Toso's (fig. 2), followed by Barbini, with whom Willson had an even more positive relationship (fig. 3). The same age as Willson, Barbini had pioneered *massiccio* animal figures in the early 1940s and exhibited them at the various Venice Biennales. One of Willson's early works, *Silver Virgin* (1970), made with Barbini, became the first work

by an American to enter a Venetian art museum, the Museo del Vetro di Murano. Eventually, Willson went on to work with other masters, including Signoretto and Roberto Moretti, because Barbini resisted Willson's pressures to make increasingly larger sculptures of solid glass.

Willson's importance cannot be overstated. Free to roam from one hot shop to another in search of the technicians who would execute his ideas as he wanted them done, Willson had the most sustained and varied presence of any of the Americans in Venice during this time, returning nearly every year until 1996. As a tribute to his successful integration into the Venetian glass and art establishment, he remains the only American to receive retrospective exhibitions at both the Museo Correr in Piazza San Marco (1968) and the Galleria Internazionale D'Arte Moderna at Ca' Pesaro (1984).

A friendly, tall figure whom the Italians likened to actor James Stewart, Willson found and cultivated the younger glassworkers he saw heading up the ladder in the complicated hot-shop hierarchy, among them Moretti, Rosin, Signoretto (who begged to be adopted by him and return with him to Texas), and Elio Raffaeli of Ars

Murano, his final factory choice. All made possible Willson's extraordinary evolution as an artist. Conversely, his example prodded the Italian masters to pursue figurative, solid-glass sculpture on their own.

Willson's entrée to Venice, following his work with the Tosos, was through Egidio Costantini, the controversial founder of La Fucina degli Angeli (The forge of the angels), a firm without its own workshop where artists such as Willson could rent space and hire glassblowers to execute their sculptures. Because he did not have his own factory, Costantini did not carry the same financial prestige, or respect, among Murano workers as did Venini and Toso. The firm's illustrious stable of artists included Jean Arp, Marc Chagall, Max Ernst, Joan Miró, Pablo Picasso, and Mark Tobey. As Costantini told this author: "My rule is that the artist prepares the drawings. That is how it happened with Robert Willson. But then I oversaw... how the glass would turn out. This is how I worked with Picasso, Miró, and the others."[13] Some of Willson's greatest works, such as *Letter of Stone* (1970), were done at La Fucina degli Angeli under such circumstances.

Whereas Willson had managed to quickly crack the Venetian social code and find a place for himself, going so far as to rent a flat across from the Accademia and to host the after-party for his 1984 Ca' Pesaro show at the spectacular Palazzo Dario, the younger Americans who followed him were on their own.

The next wave consisted of Chihuly, Marquis, Carpenter, Lipofsky, and Dailey, each of whom separately approached de Santillana about working at Venini and was accepted. By the time of Chihuly's Fulbright sojourn in 1968-1969, Marquis' in 1969-1970, and Dailey's in 1972-1973, word was getting out that even if one could not actually work at the hot shop, it was worth the visit just to observe the team process and to learn whom one could approach there for whatever needed to be done.

Chihuly's encounters with Venice came at the beginning and middle of his career, first as de Santillana's unthreatening mascot, who was allowed to watch and design a few maquettes for lamps that were never put into production, and then later as the budding American celebrity artist on his honeymoon who turned to the forbidden Fascist period of Venetian glass for his important and ongoing body of work, the *Venetians* series begun in 1988 (plates 56, 57, 58, 60, 61). In these works, with the help of Italian artisans such as Tagliapietra and Signoretto, Chihuly replenished the Mussolini-era, quasimachine aesthetic of Martens, Martinuzzi, and others with greater scale, brighter color, and subtle surface adornments. As we shall see, his efforts in rehabilitating the blown vessel led to an influx of Italians to his Pilchuck Glass School in Stanwood, Washington, near Seattle. Tagliapietra, Signoretto, Ongaro, and Rosin were all invited by Chihuly, and they subsequently changed the face of American glass art. Tagliapietra in particular became the new Christopher Columbus discovering America.

Chihuly's 1996 extravaganza *Chihuly over Venice* outdid Willson's earlier Venice exhibitions, and his cultivation of relationships with Venetian authorities (including remunerations when needed) made the vast indoor and outdoor displays of his *Chandeliers* possible. With the *Chandeliers*, which were installed in fourteen locations throughout Venice, Chihuly's revivalist affinities shifted from the Fascist style to the 17th-century glory days of the Baroque. Multiplying blown curlicues by the hundreds and clustering them around invisible metal armatures, he emulated and gently satirized the over-the-top ornate lighting fixtures that had become (and still are) a major export item for Murano; yet his *Chandeliers* relied on exterior rather than interior light sources.

Palazzo Ducale Chandelier (1996) is unique in that it operates in close tandem with a preexisting glass architectural element: a historic glass chandelier within the Doge's Palace. This one work encapsulates the juxtaposition of old and new, Italian and American, rigid tradition and freedom of expression. Its dazzling technique and composition rival the original. It also symbolizes the growing differences between "old Europe" and the imperializing tendencies of American culture and military power. Chihuly "conquered" Venice, if only for one month in August 1996.

Marquis, when he arrived in Venice in 1969 as the next Fulbright scholar, worked first at Salviati & C. for two weeks before shifting to Venini. There he saw Ongaro make *murrine*—cut, colored glass cane sections of a salami-like strand of hot glass rod—which changed Marquis' entire approach to glass (fig. 4). With his stipend extended into 1970, at the height of the Vietnam War and the American intervention into Cambodia, Marquis created numerous glass sculptures using various types of murrine (plate 53). Intended as a criticism of the U.S. government's policies in Vietnam, these works constitute the first examples of political glass art made in Venice. Marquis unwittingly neutralized the cold authority of Mussolini-era glass, reinvigorating glass with newly expressive powers of social protest.

Carpenter was a cofounder of Pilchuck in 1971 and collaborated with Chihuly on numerous large-scale architectural projects between 1970 and 1974. In 1971-1972, he worked at Venini, where he both observed and made several designs that were put into limited production. Carpenter went on to become a highly successful architectural-glass designer in New York, executing projects throughout the world.

Lipofsky arrived in the summer of 1972 and, like Marquis, spent two weeks at Salviati & C. before switching over to Venini. This visit marked the beginning of an equally long and complicated series of relationships between

Lipofsky and numerous international teams hired to make his glass. Many U.S. glass artists strayed beyond Venice to work in other European and Asian venues (Willson was also in France and the Netherlands; Chihuly in Ireland, the Czech Republic, and Finland), but Lipofsky is the unlettered "ambassador of glass," making a point to go to far-off places such as Croatia, Korea, Turkey, and Japan to create his series of asymmetrical, bulbous sculptures. Lipofsky's continent-hopping has tended to overshadow the singularity of his Italian periods, but they provide a crucial example of how he was able to get the best work possible out of his Italian colleagues and hot-shop crews. Italy prepared Lipofsky for the world beyond Murano.

The Berkeley-based former student of Littleton (as was Chihuly) did much of the blowing himself as well as in collaboration, frequently in Venice, with Gianni Toso (fig. 5). (Toso was, strictly speaking, the first Italian glass artist invited to the West Coast by Lipofsky in 1976. The two worked closely during that visit, and Toso returned again in 1977 and 1983.) Lipofsky's signature shapes—open-form hemispheres that followed on the organic and visceral imagery of Bay Area Funk art—were executed in

a number of series at Venini, taking advantage of the bright colors and superior technical skills available there. Amusingly, *Venini Series 1972 #7* (1972) is clear glass, with red, white, and blue stripes (plate 47). It echoes the more overt aspect of Americana in Marquis' murrine pieces made around this same time out of cut-glass caning sections.

Lipofsky was at an advantage upon arriving in Venice in having already worked at the Vetreria Buzzoni in Gessatta, with Roberto Niederer in 1972, where he executed several "large glass sculptures."[14] He had also been invited by Toso, whom he met in Zürich at the first International Glass Symposium in 1972, to work in his Venice studio, but they ended up working together at Venini instead and continued a collaborative relationship for the next 30 years—the longest-lasting connection to a single Murano master among the Americans. Also in 1972, Lipofsky "crossed the canal to the Seguso factory and blew some small glass pieces" for himself. In 1976, Toso returned "home" to Fratelli Toso, where the two made sculptures together.

Dailey, another Fulbright scholar, discovered a career-changing form while working in Venice: the blown-glass lamp fitted into a metal or bronze armature. By the time he left, late in 1973, after staying about a year, he had created 25 lamps and embarked on a longer series with greater variations for which he is best known today (plates 45, 46).

Moore, who arrived at Venini in 1978, became the crucial linguistic link between Italian and American glassmakers. While in Venice, he focused on mastering the skills needed to create another prized hallmark of Venetian glass—the thin wall—in the process giving new meaning to the old Italian adage, *Il traduttore è un traditore* (the translator is a traitor).[15] Moore's proto-types failed to be accepted into production at Venini, even though de Santillana had hired him as a designer, placing him on an under-the-table retainer. They got along well together, the sophisticated director-owner and the eager, bilingual young American. Telling jokes in Italian and impressing the Venetians with his quickly gained knowledge of fine Italian wines, Moore meshed perfectly, moving easily between elegant dinners in palazzi with the de Santillanas and Sunday lunches at coworkers' homes on Murano Island.

Paolo Venini's daughter, Anna, who married de Santillana, said in later years that she regretted the most important cultural interchange in Venetian glass in the 20th century, that between the Americans and the Italians:

At first I looked favourably on this exchange. Now, however, I wonder if we were not a little too generous, since that openness perhaps entailed losing our heritage of experience and knowl-edge.... [T]he benefits had been heavily in favour of those who had come,... they had effectively taken away more than they had brought.[16]

This somewhat startling comment must be seen in the ironic context that both of her children, Laura and Alessandro, went to the United States, where they established themselves as successful artists before returning to live in Venice. Laura de Santillana's and Alessandro Diaz de Santillana's contributions are a major part of the reciprocal arrangements benefiting both American and Italian glass artists.

As we shall see below, the caravan of Italians that began with the two brothers-in-law, Lino and Checco, and their wives (who continued to disagree for years over the wisdom of letting the New World in on the secrets of Murano glass) was but a trickle at first, barely commented upon in Venice, although critics such as Tagliapietra's brother, Silvano, an art critic and newspa-per editor, had been warning for a decade that the tight-knit community "produced and sold [glass] as if it were potatoes."[17] Obviously, for many, Venice was long overdue for an influx of new ideas even before the arrival of the Americans and the exodus of the Italians to the United States.

Tina Aufiero succeeded Moore as resident guest designer at Venini, with consecutive stays in 1983 and 1984, overlapping with Zynsky in the spring of 1984. Both artists had better luck than their male compatriot in creating designs that actually went into production. Zynsky was living at the time in Amsterdam, where she had invented, with Mathijs Teunissen van Manen, in 1982, the use of *filet de verre*, colored glass thread slumped over a vessel mold, a technique for which she gained international acclaim. Like Willson, she garnered European approval before cracking the fickle American market with her uniquely colorful, bowl-like sculptures (plate 83).[18] Aufiero and Zynsky prepared the way in Venice for another American artist, Ginny Ruffner, who had a successful, if temporarily ill-fated, residency at Vistosi in 1989.

As Tina Oldknow has described the events, Ruffner's stay at Vistosi to make fourteen sculptures and one chandelier was erased from the artist's memory when she awoke in 1991 from a five-week coma resulting from a head-on car collision in North Carolina.[19] Four years later, a group of American glass art collectors headed by Pilchuck Glass School executive director Marjorie Levy was invited by an American expatriate in Venice, Louise Berndt, to visit Maurizio Albarelli's showroom. The Vistosi com-pany had been sold to Albarelli in 1985, and, among the remaining inventory, he kept 50 preparatory drawings and watercolors and the 15 glassworks that emerged out of Ruffner's project. Eight years after they were made, these works were seen for the first time in the United States, to wide acclaim, at Meyerson & Nowinski, in Seattle. Their complex compositions (executed by Pino Signoretto's brother, Silvano), bright solid colors, and graceful balance immediately strengthened Ruffner's reputation as a sculptor in glass.

She still insists that "the drawings and sculptures were never really forgotten. It's just that I had other priorities."[20] "What happened to Ruffner in Venice is a remarkable story—a mystery that was solved by art collectors on vacation, a memory that was restored to the artist who had "forgotten" it, and the display of a body of work that added immeasurably to the record of Americans in Venice. Oldknow's close reading of Ruffner's Surrealist-derived imagery accords them the serious analysis they deserve. With the Ruffner-Vistosi collaboration restored to Venetian glass art history, the picture of excellence in both Italian and American glass sculpture became clearer once again.

Italians in America

In the summer of 1978, at Moore's invitation, Ongaro spent a few weeks teaching at the Pilchuck Glass School. Ongaro had already been to San Francisco in 1973, but the Pilchuck visit (which he made with his wife, Rina) put into motion an important reciprocal cultural interchange that changed not only American glass art but also, conceivably, American craft overall to the effect that it helped push glass to the top of the craft-

media hierarchy, supplanting ceramic vessels and sculpture. The rise of glass in the 1990s is directly related to the new skills and expertise transmitted to the Americans by the Italians, beginning in the 1970s.

Signora Ongaro did not like America or the hearty, rustic food at Pilchuck. And she had concerns about what her neighbors in the glass community would think about her husband's being paid by a wealthy American timber magnate (John H. Hauberg, a cofounder of Pilchuck, which was built on his land) to explain and demonstrate complicated Murano technical secrets to American college students.[21] As a result, the Ongaros did not return to Pilchuck the following year but, instead, sent by his wife, Lina. Tagliapietra's residency let loose the dam of thirteen generations of family glassblowing knowledge, which he enthusiastically shared with his students (fig. 6).

Of all the Italians who came to America in the 1970s and 1980s, Tagliapietra by far had the greatest impact.[22] He visited the United States repeatedly, beginning in 1979, and eventually acquired a home in Seattle, along with a 6,000-square-foot storage facility, office, and showroom. Tagliapietra's example of sharing information and expertise won the hearts of his many students at Pilchuck and elsewhere. Looking back at the situation in Venice that drove him to find a new creative freedom in America, he commented:

I was born on the Rio de Vetrai, the "glassblower's channel," in Murano but, in America, I became a better artist. The importance of America to me is giving me incredible opportunity to be free. Freedom! It's a very philosophical question.... I had a lot of curiosity.... [In Italy], when I designed something, it was all with production in mind. Now, I make what I want.[23]

And discussing what he found in America, he was polite:

There was a little bit of shock—and frustration. I saw the incredible energy but the teaching level was very low. And then, at Pilchuck, I was trying to do reticello but the glass quality was very low. Now [28 years later], if I want something, the very next day, I have it.

Tagliapietra is the epitome of the Italo-American cultural interchange. He even credits Chihuly with helping him to construct a career as an artist, including assistance with photography of his work and setting up relationships with dealers. He disputes Anna Venini's accusations of cultural espionage on the part of the Americans: "Anna Venini, she made a big mistake. She got much more back from America than America [took] from her."

Tagliapietra's art changed in America, becoming more technically daring, with long, flaring necks on his vases, more colorful, and, in general, reflective of a more fully individual aesthetic. The necks of his vases were sometimes up to three feet long, as in the *Dinosaurs* (1997–)

(fig. 6) Bryan Rubino (left) and Dante Marioni (second from left) watch as Lino Tagliapietra (right) creates a stemmed goblet at Pilchuck Glass School in 1992.

(plate 116). Once the demand for his own art increased, Tagliapietra also took advantage of the skill availability back in Murano, hiring, for example, experts...on the lightly hammered and chipped surfaces called *battuto*. His works are often a medley of such techniques, all subsumed within a graceful profile.

With a string of successful gallery and museum exhibitions in Florida, New York, Seattle, Japan, and elsewhere, Tagliapietra is quick to credit American collectors as well for his good fortune: "They support everything." But, he adds, "The schools and teachers are key.... The young Americans deserve better teachers."

Before Ongaro's short-lived stay in America and Tagliapietra's much smoother transition, Willson had encouraged Moretti to work at Pilgrim Glass in West Virginia. The latter's sojourn there in the early 1970s went unnoticed, but it ranks with Gianni Toso's 1976 California College of Arts and Crafts workshop as a precedent for the Italian invasions at Pilchuck Glass School by Tagliapietra, Signoretto, and Rosin.

Rosin spent the summer of 1988, followed by subsequent visits over the next few years, in the United States, coming with his brother, Dino, to teach a special class at Pilchuck on massiccio (fig. 7). Previously groomed by Willson as early as 1970, when he was affiliated with Costantini and La Fucina degli Angeli, Rosin was pushed by Willson to test the pipe's limits for holding large blobs of glass. Rosin's own work shared Willson's taste for human figures. Rosin was tragically killed in a Jet Ski accident in Venice at the age of 55. Had he lived longer, he no doubt would have developed further; his death was a tangible loss to a Murano culture in the process of taking greater creative risks, at the urging of the Americans.

Signoretto observed: "Whenever I tried to get beyond a certain point [in Murano], there was always a wall created by those before me.... They would say, 'You can't do this; you're not supposed to try that.'" [24]

And it is worth remembering that, like Rosin, he, too, had been "discovered" by Willson. When Barbini became reluctant to make the increasingly larger sculptures that Willson wanted, he passed Willson on to one of his younger protégés, Signoretto, who recalled: "That was fantastic! To have my old maestro send someone to me! I had seen my maestro make them and then later I got to make them!" [25]

Signoretto's new shop was already in operation when he met Willson in 1983, five years before his first visit to Pilchuck (followed by visits in 1989, 1990–1996, and 2003) (fig. 8). Working with Willson, Signoretto expanded his abilities so that, when he was asked by Chihuly to make the solid-glass cherubs or putti appended to the early *Venetians*, he was completely comfortable and more than competent to fulfill the American's requests. Later work for New York artist Jeff Koons, along with exhibitions of his own work in the United States, also helped establish Signoretto's reputation as the top Venetian glassblower to go to for sculptural works.

Finally, Signoretto's respective relationships to U.S. and Italian glass have, after eighteen years, struck the most sensible balance of all. His example provides a new paradigm for future Muranese contemplating a continuation of what has been—detractors notwithstanding—an entirely positive and necessary cultural interchange. Recalling the creative roadblocks he faced in Italy,

As we have seen, the reciprocal nature of the cultural interchange between Italian and American glass artists was not always equally weighted. Early on, the Americans were more indebted to the Italians, whose transfer of expertise helped the Americans improve upon and realize their ambitious dreams. At the same time, the Italians were exposed to the more open society and greater economic opportunities available in the United States. On both sides, the translators were transformed not into traitors but into global citizens.

For the future, in a time of vanishing national borders within the European Union coupled with a parallel fear of losing national cultural traditions, the Italo-American glass experience may serve as a positive model. Both countries benefited and both traditions were renovated to better achieve the innovations without which no tradition can endure.

(fig. 7) Loredano Rosin (left) and Dino Rosin (right) at Pilchuck Glass School in 1988.

(fig. 8) Pino Signoretto demonstrating at Pilchuck Glass School in 1992.

1 See Serge Guilbaut, *How New York Stole the Idea of Modern Art: Abstract Expressionism, Freedom and the Cold War* for one view (Chicago: University of Chicago Press, 1983), and Frances Stonor Saunders, *The Cultural Cold War: The CIA and the World of Arts and Letters* for another (New York: New Press, 1999).

2 See, for example, Lawrence Alloway, "The Arts and Mass Media," *Architectural Design* (February 1958), and "Pop Art: The Words," in Alloway, *Topics in American Art Since 1945* (New York: Norton, 1975), 119.

3 Elaine Levin, *The History of American Ceramics 1607 to the Present: From Pipkins and Bean Pots to Contemporary Forms* (New York: Abrams, 1988), 216-217.

4 See my *Robert Willson: Image-maker* (San Antonio: Pace-Willson Foundation; Seattle: University of Washington Press, 2001).

5 See Jutta Page, *Beyond Venice: Glass in the Venetian Style, 1500-1700* (Corning, NY: Corning Museum of Glass; New York: Hudson Hills Press, 2004).

6 See especially Rosa Barovier Mentasti, "A Millennium of Venetian Glassmaking," in *Venetian Glass 1890–1990* (Venice: Arsenale, 1992), and Marino Barovier, "The Art of Glass on Murano," in *Murano: Glass from the Olnick Spanu Collection* (New York: Millennium Pictures, 2003), 14–24. This new scholarship makes up for the oversight of earlier omnibus histories, such as Giovanni Mariacher, *L'Arte del Vetro* (Milan: Mondadori, 1954), which made no mention of the Americans.

7 Norman Kogan, *A Political History of Postwar Italy* (New York: Praeger, 1966), 24.

8 See Marina Barovier et al., *Napoleone Martinuzzi: Vetraio del Novecento* (Venice: Il Cardo, 1992).

9 William Warmus, "The Venetians," in *The Venetians: Modern Glass, 1919-1990* (New York: Muriel Karasik Gallery, 1989), 6.

10 Mentasti, "A Millennium of Venetian Glassmaking" 142.

11 See Marilynn Johnson et al., *Louis Comfort Tiffany: Artist for the Ages* (New York: Scala, 2005).

12 "From a boat/Venice is where/Houses grow out of the water/People walk on waves/All the young girls/Who are so rounded./It cannot be real." Robert Willson, translated into Italian by Marguerite Shore, copyright © Pace-Willson Foundation, 2001.

13 Egidio Costantini, interview with the author, Venice, March 13, 2001.

14 Marvin Lipofsky, conversation with author, August 10, 2006. All other Lipofsky quotations are from this source.

15 See my "Benjamin Moore: The Translator," in *Craft and Concept: The Rematerialization of the Art Object* (New York: Midmarch Arts, 2006), 272.

16 Anna Venini Diaz de Santillana, "The Venini Glassworks 1921-1986: A Passion for Glass," in *Venini Catalogue Raisonné 1921-1986*, 53.

17 [Silvano Tagliapietra] "Le sculture in vetro di Robert Willson," *La Voce di Murano 4*, no. 26 (August 1968): 1.

18 See my "Toots Zynsky: The Climate of Color," in *Craft and Concept*, 196.

19 Tina Oldknow, "Ginny Ruffner: Venice Rediscovered," in *Ginny Ruffner: Venice Works, 1989* (Seattle: Meyerson & Nowinski Art Associates, 1997), 12.

20 Ibid.

21 Benjamin Moore, interview with author, Seattle, August 18, 2006.

22 Tagliapietra has been the subject of numerous published interviews and monographs, including Giovanni Sarpellon, *Lino Tagliapietra: Vetri* (Venice: Arsenale, 1994), and Daniel Kany, *Lino Tagliapietra: Maestro* (Sun Valley, Idaho: Friesen Gallery, 2005).

23 Lino Tagliapietra, interview with author, Seattle, July 16, 2006. All subsequent quotations are from this source.

24 Tina Oldknow, *Pilchuck: A Glass School* (Seattle: University of Washington Press, 1996), 231.

25 See my *Robert Willson: Image-maker*, 80.

The Italian Connection: Americans at Venini

SUSANNE K. FRANTZ

ART THAT IS SOPHISTICATED IN BOTH DESIGN AND execution and formed of hot glass outside of the commercial factory setting is not difficult to find today, but that was hardly the case 50 years ago. In the United States at that time, it was almost impossible for an artist or independent craftsperson to have access to molten glass. Opportunities for hands-on experience within the glass industry were rare and usually limited to visits to the rapidly mechanizing tableware factories of Ohio and West Virginia. Following Harvey Littleton's pioneering efforts at the University of Wisconsin, where he was a professor of ceramics, and at the Toledo Museum of Art early in the 1960s, a handful of American university art departments began to incorporate glass-blowing into their programs. Both faculty and students, however, were essentially self-taught and finding their own ways—a situation that would persist for several years to come.

Students who sought advanced technical expertise looked to the ancient glassmaking traditions of Europe,

and many were befriended by a single company operating on the island of Murano in the Venetian Lagoon, the very heart of Italian glassmaking. The encounter of American studio glass artists with Italy's most experimental glassworks, Venini & C., coincided with the installation of a new visionary to head that firm: Ludovico Diaz de Santillana, an architect and the son-in-law of founder Paolo Venini. De Santillana was an outsider to Murano and first entered that insular glassmaking community through marriage to one of Venini's daughters, Anna. He never intended to be a businessman or to manage a glass factory, and was in the process of moving his family to Cambridge, Massachusetts, where he was to assume a teaching position at the Massachusetts Institute of Technology, when Paolo Venini died prematurely in 1959. De Santillana assumed leadership of the company with his mother-in-law, Ginette.

Venini had established the precedent of inviting distinguished foreign artists to design for the company in the late 1930s, when he hired the Swedish ceramist Tyra Lundgren. The first Americans to work at the small

factory/large workshop were Eugene Berman, Kenneth George Scott, and Charles Lin Tissot in the 1950s (see the chronology of American artists at Venini on page 32).[1] Berman was a painter who had emigrated from Russia to the United States in the 1930s. At Venini, he created a new product line of sculptural objects based on architectural motifs. Industrial designer and painter Scott lived in Paris immediately following World War II, subsequently moving to Milan to enter the fashion industry. His series of solid glass fish commissioned by Macy's department store in New York was produced at Venini in 1951 (plate 24). Beginning in the mid-1950s, Tissot had decorative items such as glass birdcages and flowers produced at Venini for Bonniers, an interior design retailer also located in Manhattan (plate 29). With very different aspirations, Littleton spent two and a half months in the late 1950s visiting Naples and Murano as part of his search for ways to make hot glass available to the American artist-artisan. Thanks to the family connections of an army buddy, Amadeo Guetta, Littleton was able to observe glassmakers at the small work, but when he asked for a chance to try his hand at blowing glass at Venini, his informal proposal was politely declined.[2]

In 1959, Oklahoma-born artist Thomas Stearns wrote to Paolo Venini asking if he might come to Murano to study glass.[3] The 24-year-old Stearns was also a painter and former student in the fibers department at the Cranbrook Academy of Art in Bloomfield Hills, Michigan. He was experienced in various craft techniques and mailed a few photographs of his experiments with kiln-fused glass panels to Murano. Venini had made his own efforts in the same direction a few years earlier and saw the potential of exploring architectural glass applications with Stearns. A postgraduate fellowship for research in glass and fiber awarded by the Italian government and a Fulbright travel grant financed the American's stay.

Venini died before Stearns arrived in Italy. Fortunately for Stearns, de Santillana also valued fresh perspectives and was committed to uniting great designers with skilled craftspeople. He was determined to build upon his father-in-law's international perspective, which was guided by the imperative to look beyond Murano for innovative ways not only to advance the family firm but also to ensure the survival of fine Italian glassmaking as a whole. Although he was unaware of the earlier agreement, de Santillana welcomed Stearns when he appeared at the door in December 1960. Unlike his American predecessors, Stearns did not come to Murano as a designer, nor did he have a desire to blow glass. Rather, he was simply fascinated by the material and curious to investigate it as a medium for his art.

The official arrangement between Stearns and the company was vague. He was given access to the entire factory and allowed to observe all phases of its operation. The nature of what he would contribute in return was left open, though de Santillana did request that at least half of Stearns' activities be directed toward potential commercial applications. The American spent time at the glass research center (Stazione Sperimentale) perusing the library and studying the collection of historic glass there and in the Venini offices. He worked daily on the factory floor and often arrived at the plant by four or five in the morning, when the annealing oven containing the previous day's output was opened. In a sense, Stearns straddled the company's two worlds of labor and management. As he worked to assimilate

(fig. 1) Thomas Stearns (right) with Francesco "Checco" Ongaro at Venini, around 1962.

himself into the routine of the factory workers, he also ate lunch frequently with de Santillana, followed by brandy and espresso in the chief executive's office. Stearns' residency at Venini would ultimately set the tone and pave the way for the young American studio glass artists who followed.

At the end of his first two weeks, Stearns turned his attention from fused glass to blown objects. His first models and sketches, including the type of sculptural off-axis vessel he created known as *Cappello del Doge* (Doge's hat) (plate 26), were soundly rejected by the revered senior glassblower, maestro Arturo Biasutto (known as "Boboli"). When Boboli refused to consider them, one of the younger masters, Francesco "Checco" Ongaro, took pity on Stearns and offered to attempt the designs (fig. 1). Despite the lack of a common language, the two men developed a successful working relationship—one of many that Ongaro would forge with foreign artists and the first with an American. Stearns' designs were "just over the edge,"[4] and Ongaro enjoyed making the quirky works that went against almost every rule in the book. The natural curiosity, graciousness, patience, and eagerness for new challenges expressed by this native Muranese became crucial to Stearns' success. Ongaro's acceptance also helped improve Stearns' relationship with other individuals, among them Paolo's widow, who were opposed to the idea of a foreigner's gaining so much in-depth knowledge of the traditional techniques.[5]

At the end of the first year, when the grants paying his expenses were exhausted, Stearns was hired by the company as a resident guest designer (although his official work permit was applied for and received only two weeks before the end of his stay). Variations on the title would be used over the following years to encompass a wide range of abilities and interests on the part of the visiting artists, as well as to confer on them some small status. Once he became a paid member of the staff, Stearns found that his opportunities expanded. Ongaro was instructed by de Santillana to interrupt his normal production work to attend to Stearns' pieces as needed. The company's color chemist on-staff duplicated the unusual hues that Stearns painted on swatches and brought in for matching. The asymmetrical and atypical shapes and moody palette were not well received by most of the work force, and Signora Venini called Stearns' selections *colori molto triste* (colors of much sadness). The new designs ranged from *incalmo* vessels that were complex and extremely difficult to fabricate, formed of multiple bubbles of hard-to-work colors such as red and metallic black joined together and blown deliberately off-center, to relatively simple and less expensive-to-produce cylindrical incalmo vases with opaque bases

and wrapped spiral decoration. Sometimes the molten glass was so dark and opaque that Ongaro called his challenge "blind blowing."[6]

Several of the less demanding vases and lampshades were introduced into the company production line (fig. 2), and though the ideas became the property of Venini, Stearns was allowed to keep a handful of representative examples. All of his most personal concepts—most notably the variations on the *Cappello del Doge;* the heavy, finely incised *Moon Mist* series meant to be held in cupped hands (Stearns estimated that fewer than fifteen were executed); the *Facades of Venice,* with vertical cane decoration (plate 27)[7]; and the monumental *Standing Sentinels*[8]—were meant to evoke the subtleties of reflected Venetian light, the striations of the murky lagoon, and the city's shadowy architecture.

Stearns was invited to stay at Venini another two years, but at the end of 1962 he returned to the United States to make sculpture of natural fibers knotted on armatures that echoed the melting shapes of his glass *Sentinels.* Although at one point he was invited to submit designs for Steuben, and for a time was placed on retainer by Venini & C. in anticipation of future collaborations, Stearns did not produce any additional glass pieces. Back in Murano, the positive critical response to Stearns' designs when they were unveiled as Venini's representation at the 1962 Venice Biennale (fig. 3), in combination

with the American's successful working relationship with Ongaro, left de Santillana feeling optimistic about receiving future visitors.

Stearns was an artist using glass, but he was not a member of what came to be known as the American studio glass movement, which had a mindset—from the 1960s and well into the 1980s—that expected designers to execute their designs without the aid of a professional craftsperson. Despite a dearth of information and slow technical progress, by 1968 some interesting sculptural glass pieces were being produced in the United States. What was then regarded as a competent level of craftsmanship—particularly for glassblowing—can in hindsight be seen as only elementary. At the same time, an awareness of the brilliant achievements of historic glassmakers (mainly via photographic reproductions), especially those of the Roman period and in Murano during the 15th and 16th centuries, drove some students to pursue a higher degree of manual skill. Like Stearns, they looked to Europe for that experience and knowledge.

The next American artist-artisan to spend an extended period of time at Venini was Dale Chihuly,[9] a 1968 recipient of a Master of Fine Arts degree from the Rhode Island School of Design (RISD), Providence. During the preceding two years, Chihuly had shifted his allegiance from interior design and textiles to glassblowing. In an estimated 100 identical letters written in Italian and sent to Muranese glass manufacturers, Chihuly enclosed three slides of his work and requested the opportunity to fulfill a Fulbright grant. The only response—positive or otherwise—to his mass mailing came from de Santillana, who granted permission for Chihuly to come to Venini.

De Santillana traveled often to New York and was keenly aware of the new developments in American studio glass.[10] Perhaps in Chihuly's inquiry, as in Stearns' before him, de Santillana saw some unknown future benefit for the Italian glass industry. Regardless, by opening the doors to an artist who was committed to the craft of glassblowing, de Santillana unwittingly affected the course of American and, ultimately, international glass art and craft. The decision was commented upon optimistically by Paul Perrot, then director of the Corning Museum of Glass and a studio glass enthusiast: "I shall be looking forward as time goes on to seeing the results from your new artist in residence. It is an extremely interesting concept and one which cannot help but be enormously attractive to the individual concerned and, I hope, beneficial to glass design in general."[11]

When Chihuly first encountered de Santillana in December 1968, he was treated to a gracious reception and a discussion in de Santillana's fluent English. Chihuly explained that he was willing to undertake any work, for no pay; the Fulbright grant would cover all his expenses. Even though the company did not incur out-of-pocket expenses, the process of bringing another untrained foreigner up to a level where he could be of any help was costly in terms of company time. Chihuly was eager to find a way in which he could be of use. When de Santillana explained that the firm was negotiating for an important sculpture commission in nearby Ferrara, Chihuly jumped at the opportunity to assist. In the United States, he had constructed sculptural environments of blown-glass components that sometimes incorporated neon, and he offered to assemble a full-scale detail from the Venini sculpture proposal. The model was formed of plastic and blown-glass spheres (made by the Venini workers), each measuring approximately 18 inches in diameter and filled with neon elements. The job was eventually awarded to Venini, although the final sculpture was never realized. Nevertheless, on the basis of this effort, Chihuly was given design studio space and access to all areas of the

(fig. 2) Undated Venini sales catalogue with image of Thomas Stearns' "Lines of Light" lamps designed around 1962.

(fig. 3) Archival photograph of the Venini display at the 31st Venice Biennale, 1962, devoted exclusively to Thomas Stearns' designs.

Left to right: *Cappello del Doge* (Doge's hat); a pair of the *Facades of Venice*; an untitled work with two top openings, known only (according to Stearns) as the "Biennale" piece; two variations on the *Cappello del Doge*, including one with vertical alignment of the incalmo bubbles. Stearns presumed that all of these pieces were destroyed in the 1972 Venini company fire.

factory. A few of Chihuly's design prototypes—variations on Carlo Scarpa's *murrine* (mosaic) cane and *battuto*-carved pieces as well as one lamp—were executed, but none went into production.

Chihuly had no assigned duties; like Stearns, he studied the collection of historic glass at Venini and also the books on Italian art in the library of the Cini Foundation. He spent most of his time watching the workers, especially senior maestro Mario Tosi (known as Mario "Grasso"). The technical expertise and dexterity of the Italian glassblowers left Chihuly and his later colleagues awestruck. He had blown glass with partners in school, but at Venini he saw tasks divided among four to six team members, which facilitated the production of larger and more complicated shapes. Although he was a respectable glassblower by American studio glass standards, Chihuly quickly recognized the rudimentary level of his abilities. He did not assist on any of the blowing teams, and he attempted to blow glass only one time at most during his tenure at Venini. He also watched glass casting, murrine cane making, cutting, grinding, and polishing. The company even had its own facilities for fabricating wood molds and metal parts for chandeliers,

Chihuly also saw how the glass batch recipe was mixed and melted—critical information for establishing a hot-glass studio back home. In the United States, glass artists were limited to a narrow range of glass colors that were compatible in their physical properties and could be used safely in combination, but at Venini, fifteen to twenty such colors were melted each day from raw ingredients.

Chihuly found de Santillana to be completely accepting and encouraging of his tentative efforts. Despite the prevailing ambivalence in the factory regarding the presence of technically inquisitive foreigners, most of the American visitors would meet with overall treatment that ranged from basic cordiality to genuine warmth. De Santillana even loaned a car to Chihuly and his mother so they might visit artists Erwin Eisch in Frauenau, Germany, and Stanislav Libenský and Jaroslava Brychtová in Železný Brod, Czechoslovakia.

Chihuly returned to the United States in the early summer of 1969, and his work did not immediately reflect any Italian stylization. With RISD student James Carpenter, he made more glass environments as well as panels of blown-glass roundels and an early series of Blanket cylinders inspired by Native American textiles. It was not until 1977 that an incubating Italian influence became apparent, when Chihuly's thin organic Baskets (also inspired by Native American objects) evolved rapidly into the more diaphanous Seaforms. The fluttering

transparency and pastel coloration of these vessels shared characteristics with the eccentric goblets produced by Artisti Barovier at the end of the 19th century and with the early 1920s designs of Vittorio Zecchin for Vetri Soffiati Muranesi Cappellin Venini & C., the forerunner of Venini & C. Since the 1980s, interpretations of the earlier 20th-century glass designs of Ercole Barovier, Fulvio Bianconi, Napoleone Martinuzzi, and Gio Ponti are detectable in Chihuly's designs.

In retrospect, it is possible to see how unsettling it must have been for the Muranese glassmaking community to have one of its most prominent firms open its doors to foreign students. This was a different matter altogether from permitting tourist groups to have a quick glimpse of the factory while in transit to the sales showrooms. And it was a far cry from the short-term hosting of an outside designer with minimal interest in the intricacies of the craft. Chihuly, like Stearns, stayed for months. Both went where they pleased and were free to absorb as much as they wanted about the glassmaking proceses. Chihuly and the succeeding studio glass artists were exposed to techniques that had taken hundreds of years to refine and were strictly guarded. De Santillana even permitted Chihuly to shoot Super 8 films of the glassmaking. According to Anna Venini Diaz de Santillana, her husband did not mind stirring up some controversy in the rather rigid environment of Murano.[12]

Unlike Stearns and Chihuly, the next American to visit Venini, Californian Richard Marquis, came with the

express objective of studying glassmaking mechanics and of making glass himself. He arrived in Italy in August 1969, and went through his own Fulbright grant orientation in Bologna before settling in Venice. There, Marquis walked around the glass showrooms and demonstration areas alongside the tourists. Hoping to gain real entrée to a factory, he turned to the Fulbright office in Rome, which arranged interviews at Salviati & C. and Venini. Marquis spent approximately two weeks at Salviati watching the workers and studying the collection, and then decided to move on and explore the possibilities at Venini. Preparing for his initial meeting with de Santillana, the nervous 24-year-old Marquis dressed up in his best outfit and prepared a short speech in Italian. In exchange for time at Venini, he offered to prepare a series of time-motion studies of the glassblowing operations with the audacious aim of improving the efficiency of production (which at the time consisted largely of chandeliers). De Santillana sat smoking his pipe and listened attentively before answering Marquis in perfect English. Amazingly, once again the director took a chance and agreed to the proposal. Marquis was introduced to the workers as a "guest designer," although his only payment was a daily hot lunch. After completing the time-motion drawings, he became more actively engaged in factory operations. Like Chihuly, he was taken aback by the level of proficiency, the variety of techniques, and the luxurious and inviting range of colors.

A typical day for Marquis began with an early morning walk across Venice and a vaporetto ride to Murano. Operations commenced at seven; there was a break around nine thirty, and perhaps a jug of wine was sent for from down the street. Lunch was served in the company cafeteria at eleven, and around two in the afternoon the blowing was finished. After that came cleanup and glass batch mixing in preparation for the following day's work. In the small studio he was provided, Marquis produced a few lamps and vessel designs. He also did drafting for a company project in India, and investigated the decorative potential of photosensitive glass for Venini production.

Marquis was fortunate to be in residence during a working visit by famed Finnish designer Tapio Wirkkala, which allowed him to observe firsthand an experienced artist, who arrived prepared with drawings, working effectively with a team of superb glassblowers. Marquis also spent hours watching Ongaro (now third maestro behind Mario Grasso and Mario Colelli) work with murrine cane and blow the larger objects. Eventually, he was permitted to assume the lowest-ranking position on a blowing team, and his presence enabled the other team members to move up a notch into a different position and thereby to improve their own skills. Marquis was one of the most advanced glassblowers in the United States, but in Italy, as he has stated, "It was a pitiful state of affairs. I was about as skilled as any 10-year-old on Murano."[13] "Some days he blew glass alone

or with another worker—perhaps during lunch or after the day's shift, when a bench was free. Ultimately, a group was assigned to help him on Friday afternoons, after completion of the week's production, when everyone was tired but still up for a challenge. Occasionally he was allowed to work with Ongaro and his team. It was of paramount importance to gain acceptance by the workers, and Marquis did what he could to fit in. The 1960s was a period of political ferment and labor disputes, and there were numerous work disruptions in the Murano factories. With the tacit understanding of de Santillana, Marquis stood with the employees during the strikes so that he might preserve his relationship with them and continue with his work.

The technique that first interested Marquis was the making of murrine canes. Although he understood the fabrication concept of bundling lengths of colored glass to form an image, and had purchased slices from American hobby shops, he had never seen it made until he was at Venini. Marquis' inferior blowing skills and "weird" designs added a degree of difficulty to the situation, but Ongaro was always kind and interested in tackling such challenges. Marquis' earliest murrine attempts consisted of a cloud, a childlike house, a star, and a single laboriously constructed word.[14] These were followed by a series of small blown vessels and objects based on the American flag that incorporated stars-and-stripes cane slices as decoration (plates 50, 53).

Toward the end of his stay, as the factory schedule became quite busy, Marquis asked if he might invite his friend Robert Naess to come from California and assist. Marquis and Naess made some more murrine, including one depicting Mickey Mouse and one with a hammer and sickle. Though his grant was extended for a second year, Marquis decided to return to the United States in June 1970. Soon after, he joined Naess and other friends in the creation of a word cane incorporating the entire Lord's Prayer. Although it could not compare with the highly detailed and painterly Franchini murrine from the 19th century, the cane represented a technical tour de force in American studio glass.

Marquis remained dedicated to exploring the possibilities of murrine, and an extended series of nonfunctional "patchwork" murrine teapots and other vessels became his signature for many years. At Venini, Marquis had paid attention to a Scarpa-designed murrine piece from the late 1940s that was on display in the company collection. Some of those designs were still in production, and Marquis remembers watching the application of their battuto-carved surfaces in the grinding shop.[15] In the second half of the 1980s, he began his *Marquiscarpa* series in tribute to the architect's designs (plate 88). Marquis placed shallow, elongated bowls of tightly packed murrine on top of tall bases in irreverent ways that could never be mistaken for true Scarpas. The *Occhi* (Eyes) murrine vessels of Tobia Scarpa (Carlo's son) from the early 1960s (plate 13) would also inspire new interpretations by Marquis some 30 years later. After undertaking the difficult occhi fabrication process with fellow American artist Dante Marioni, Marquis appreciated why so few examples were originally produced.[16]

James Carpenter was an undergraduate student in architecture at RISD who became an experienced glassblower by working first with Ian Nelson and then with Chihuly, who had just returned from Italy. Around 1970, Carpenter began collaborating with Chihuly on blown-glass environments, including one installed in 1971 at New York's Museum of Contemporary Crafts (now the Museum of Arts and Design). Carpenter was equally dedicated to three goals: mastering the craft of glass-blowing, gaining experience as an industrial designer, and making sculpture. After the New York exhibition closed, Carpenter wrote to de Santillana asking if he might spend his senior year at Venini as part of the RISD European Honors program. In what Carpenter remembers as "a generous gesture," the director assented and even provided a small stipend.[17] Because of his higher level of proficiency, Carpenter spent his mornings assisting on the team of Mario Grasso and came to consider himself an apprentice of that great master. On lunch hours, Carpenter was permitted to make his own pieces, with suggestions from Grasso, and during the afternoons he worked on various architectural lighting designs. The seriousness and enthusiasm demonstrated by Carpenter toward all aspects of the operation earned him the regard of both the workers and de Santillana.[18]

Carpenter was unusual in that after presenting his proposals on paper, he could walk into the blowing room and demonstrate how to execute the design. Every couple of weeks, the director would review Carpenter's ideas, and he became the first of the American artists following Stearns to have designs accepted into the Venini production line.[19] Between 1975 and 1984, he would present design proposals to the company on several more occasions.

When Carpenter returned from Italy in 1972, he brought back glassmaking tools and shared what he had learned with other American students. When he was at Venini, he had to practice proper centering and introduction of the bubble into the solid glass gathered at the end of the pipe. He encountered better ways to join sections of glass and saw the great potential of using molds. Like Chihuly before him, Carpenter became fully convinced in Murano of the superior results possible when working with a multimember team. Most important, he observed countless small movements that allowed the glass to be worked with more fluidity. At RISD, before he went to Italy, Carpenter had experimented with a way to entrap a ring of air inside the bubble of glass—a traditional technique he discovered in early Venetian glassware. After he refined this method with the experts at Venini, the effect became briefly known in America as the "RISD ridge" or the "RISD ring."

The techniques and processes that Carpenter demonstrated in the 1970s for students at RISD and at the newly founded Pilchuck Glass School in Washington State were thought to represent a comprehensive summary of Italian glassblowing skills and soon spread throughout the country. Carpenter encouraged American students to switch from what was described as the Swedish-English method of shaping the molten blob of glass with a carved wood "block" to the Italian style, known as "marvering," which involved rolling the glass on a metal plate. This technique allowed specific areas of the hot glass to be cooled by contact with the plate, which in turn allowed larger objects to be blown. In fact, Italian glassblowers used both techniques, but marvering soon gained precedence among American glass artists. Not until the late 1970s, when they could observe the dexterity of the Italian masters first-hand at Pilchuck, would the students emulate Muranese methods with a greater degree of accuracy.[20]

In the western United States, Marquis' experiences in Italy were becoming well known. Two other Californians, Michael Nourot and John Milner, wished to establish hot-glass studios and decided that a trip to Murano was the proper way to educate themselves. An acquaintance arranged a letter of introduction to de Santillana, and in June 1972 they were given a bench at Venini at which to work. Like their predecessors, the visitors were immediately humbled by the surrounding talent. They spent twelve to sixteen hours each day simply observing the factory activities; as always, Ongaro patiently answered questions and assigned small tasks to the Americans. Nourot and Milner were surprised by the high quality of the glass and the expanse of support equipment. Nourot was particularly fascinated with the pot furnaces, which melted glass quickly and efficiently; in American studios, the design of choice was a less effective day-tank furnace, which was relatively easy to build and maintain. Due to a similar lack of expertise, most Americans were condemned to blow a low-quality, resistant material produced by remelting crushed glass cullet rather than high-quality glass made from raw ingredients.[21]

Like Stearns and Chihuly, Nourot was a serious student of the company's glass collection and was devastated, as was everyone, when the building housing the offices and the historic objects burned to the ground in 1972. The day after the fire was spent digging through the debris, with production resuming the next morning. After Nourot and Milner dissolved their partnership, the former, running low on funds, considered returning home, but Ongaro secured him temporary employment with the understanding that Nourot would have to prove himself. To that end, Nourot spent four weeks climbing ladders and running with loads of glass in one of the factory's lowest positions. He later acted as a fill-in member for any team that required assistance, and at the end of his shift, he would stay on to watch the batch master prepare the next day's glass melt. In Nourot's

case, his preempting of jobs that could have been held by an Italian initially made him unpopular with his coworkers, but he eventually established his place and work on his own pieces after the end of production and before the nightly closing of the factory. Even as he was gaining the knowledge he sought, he was eager to establish his own operation, and so he returned to the United States in May 1973. He had a studio built to include a pot furnace so he could melt the basic glass formulas that were generously given to him at Venini. Following his Italian experience, Nourot began to create contemporary designs for tableware and decorative objects that contrasted with the Art Nouveau-inspired styles that were popular among other San Francisco Bay Area studio glassmakers.

At the beginning of his stay at Venini, Nourot overlapped briefly with his teacher Marvin Lipofsky, an assistant professor at the University of California, Berkeley. Lipofsky had met de Santillana in 1970, at a meeting of the International Commission on Glass in Växjö, Sweden. An invitation to visit Venini was extended to Lipofsky, who had a keen interest in factory operations, and he accepted in 1972. Lipofsky had also recently met the accomplished Muranese glassblower Gianni Toso, who had left the industry to open his own studio for artistic flameworking. Toso helped Lipofsky find a place to live, and after the latter's difficult first efforts at blowing

glass with one of the Venini workers, Toso volunteered, and was permitted, to assist. Toso and Lipofsky worked together for about one week on largely improvised designs. After rummaging through the vast array of metal molds, many for lighting devices, Lipofsky used them to shape his work for the first time. He incorporated brilliant color and lengths of decorative murrine cane into the forms. Lipofsky's time in Italy was brief, although he did return in 1975 and encouraged his students to visit.

Before Nourot departed, another American arrived for an extended stay. Glassblower Dan Dailey had just finished graduate school at RISD; his goal was to be a designer and see his ideas incorporated into industrial production. Chihuly's stories about Italy and Carpenter's letters from Murano had convinced Dailey to go there too, and in what was becoming standard procedure, he wrote to 50 Italian factories, enclosing a résumé, images of his work, and a statement in Italian. Of the thirteen replies, three were positive, including de Santillana's. Dailey used a Fulbright grant to travel to Venini in autumn 1972. Arriving the week after the tragic fire, he was warmly received and admitted to the factory, where he spent his first days helping to clean up the devastation. De Santillana's only admonition was not to interfere with normal company production.

Dailey was aware of Venini's reputation as the most innovative of the Italian glasshouses, and from conversations with de Santillana, he picked up on the director's spirit of adventurousness and receptivity to fresh ideas. Dailey admired the liveliness of contemporary Italian furniture and aimed to bring a similar quality to his own unusual glass designs while remaining true to the Venini tradition. During the 1970s, a good deal of Venini's production was devoted to lighting; therefore, Dailey designed a series of table lamps (plates 45, 46). Dailey and Ongaro did most of the blowing, and the metal fittings were fabricated in the company shop. Dailey made regular presentations on his progress to de Santillana, and everyone from the director to the fellow who swept the floor felt free to voice an opinion about the American's work. For his final review, Dailey set up a display of approximately 25 lamps. He recalls that when the director was shown the illuminated objects, he walked around silently and looked at them for a full ten to fifteen minutes before smacking his forehead and announcing, "These are mad!"[22] Dailey thought the pieces were harmonious with the Venini aesthetic, but to de Santillana's eyes, they were strange indeed. He explained to Dailey why the designs were unsuitable for production, but at the same time he was intrigued by them and kept half of the prototypes (as was his privilege) for future consideration.

Although it is unfortunate that the lamps, as with most of the designs by the inexperienced Americans, were never commercially produced, the experience was key in the development of Dailey's future work. He came to rely on the method of working with industry that he

developed at Venini, and he believes that his subsequent lighting designs evolved from his time in Murano.[23]

As a glassmaker, Dailey later employed not only Italian blowing techniques but also finishing methods, such as battuto grinding, which leaves the surface of the glass both slightly matte and slightly polished. Later, Dailey sometimes reinterpreted this technique with the use of sandblasting and acid polishing. When Dailey left Venini in 1973 for Boston to develop the glass program at the Massachusetts College of Art, he came away with more than just technical information. De Santillana and his wife had become close personal friends, having invited Dailey into their home, taken him to exhibitions, taught him the history of Italian glass, and introduced him to Vivaldi and fine wine.

William Prindle was the next American to spend time at Venini. He had taken glassblowing classes from Chihuly and Fritz Dreisbach during the course of his undergraduate work in the RISD sculpture department. When he went to Italy for his senior year, he devoted the first half of his study of bronze casting in Rome, but was aware of Venini through Chihuly and Carpenter. Although he had no idea what opportunities might be available, Prindle telephoned de Santillana and beginning in January 1974 embarked on a path very similar to that of his American predecessors. Arriving at Venini, he did odd jobs, helped on various blowing teams, blew his own pieces on lunch breaks, and tried to integrate himself into the life of the factory. Despite the nation-

wide tensions between labor and management of the period, Prindle noted the pride the workers took in their association with Venini.

After his first six months of "floating" around the operation and having gained de Santillana's admiration for some of his furniture designs, Prindle was given the opportunity to spend the summer working in Bologna, where he met Carlo Scarpa. Prindle returned to Venini in September 1974 to work on architectural lighting, and he devoted the winter of 1975 to devising steel molds to the shape of ceiling and wall fixtures, table lamps, and other items. None of his designs went into production, but Prindle sold Venini the rights to a chemical coloring system that he had developed while studying at RISD.

As a student, Prindle had discovered how little was published, especially in English, on Italian (or any) glass-making techniques. With the permission of de Santillana and the workers, he took black-and-white photographs and notes documenting the steps in the various processes, including the batching and melting procedures that could be recorded only by staying up all night in the factory.[24] Prindle hoped to produce a book with this material; however, the publishers that he and de Santillana approached felt it was too specialized to be commercially successful. Abridged sections of the texts and a few of Prindle's photos from Venini were published as a series of four articles entitled "Unusual Hot Glass Techniques" in *Glass Art* magazine during 1976 and 1977.

Although he did not go to Murano intending to become an industrial designer, Prindle soon realized that he had an affinity for that role. He learned ways of transforming ideas into feasible production by observing other designers, including Wirkkala and Carpenter; from de Santillana he learned that good design is timeless and international. Prindle saw the efficiency of starting with simplified "guerrilla" design and production—working quickly to make prototypes and solve problems before investing time and money in full-blown tooling up. Shortly after returning to the States in June 1975, Prindle entered the graduate industrial design program at RISD.

By the time that Benjamin Moore arrived at Venini in September 1978, a decade after Chihuly, the American studio glass movement had matured considerably.[25] Student glassblowing skills were at a higher level, thanks largely to the information brought back from Venini and from Swedish and Dutch factories. Moore had just graduated from RISD and was education coordinator at the young Pilchuck Glass School. He presented de Santillana with a concise design proposal, accompanied by the usual offer to undertake any task. Moore was one of the best glassblowers in the United States, but at Venini he qualified only for the lowest position on Ongaro's team. As such, he spent his first year in Murano opening and closing molds, carrying pieces to the annealing oven, and running errands.[26] Like the Americans who preceded him at Venini, Moore possessed a limited ability to speak Italian, but to the amusement of the workers, he picked up the Venetian dialect and insisted on speaking it rather than pure Italian. Ongaro became a mentor, and Moore spent much of his free time with the maestro's family.

Moore strove continually to improve his glassmaking skills by emulating the masters around him. He observed that the temperature at which the molten glass was blown was much hotter than he was accustomed to, and that an object was kept very hot until it was finished. The extreme temperatures permitted the glass to be blown to a remarkable thinness. Moore was fortunate also to have the opportunity to work on Mario Grasso's team for approximately two weeks, but it took months of watching before he was able to fully comprehend the subtle efficiency and effortlessness of Grasso's immense skill. Moore hoped to eventually establish his own studio in the Pacific Northwest modeled on the practices and standards of excellence he found at Venini.

Halfway through the year, Ongaro offered to execute some of Moore's designs. They put together a body of work, and de Santillana was sufficiently impressed to ask the American to return as a designer in the fall, after Moore's summer back at Pilchuck. Moore asked Ongaro to join him at the school and spend a few weeks demonstrating Italian glassmaking techniques, which he did. Ongaro had already been to the United States around 1973; although he had visited some San Francisco Bay Area glass studios, he had never taught outside Murano until the 1978 session at Pilchuck (fig. 4). Moore returned to Venini in September and stayed through May 1979. When he invited Ongaro to teach a second summer at Pilchuck, the maestro declined, but recommended his brother-in-law, Lino Tagliapietra, a master who had worked at Venini from 1966 to 1968 and was now head of design and production at another Muranese glass factory, Effetre International. The first American glassmakers that Tagliapietra met were Nourot and Milner, but by 1979 he knew several of the foreign artists and immediately jumped at the opportunity to visit the United States for the first time. Since that initial trip and in tandem with his later decision to work freelance, Tagliapietra has taught worldwide and evolved into an acclaimed artist.[27]

All of the Americans who followed Stearns to Venini were glass artisans as well as artists. While all were aware of the special opportunity that Murano offered to improve their skills, each arrived with different goals in mind. Some were interested primarily in gleaning information, learning techniques, and improving their manual skills. Others desired more experience as designers, with hopes of seeing their work put into commercial production. Unlike the earlier Americans, who had approached the company hat in hand willing to take on any task, the last two artists to spend time at Venini while it was still partially under family ownership, RISD graduates Tina Aufiero and Toots Zynsky, were asked

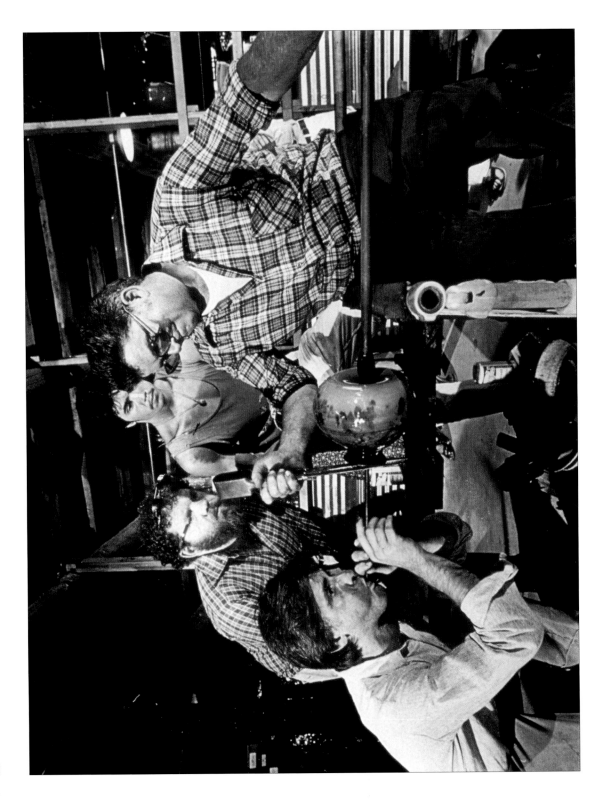

(fig. 4) Checco Ongaro (right) assisted by Benjamin Moore (far left) at the Pilchuck Glass School, 1978; background: Dale Chihuly and William Morris. Pictured in *Heir Apparent: Translating the Secrets of Venetian Glass*, Bellevue Art Museum, Washington, 1997.

by de Santillana to work in a slightly different capacity. Both were given formalized contracts to work on company projects as well as to make their own sculptures using the company's facilities.

When Aufiero first visited Murano in October 1982, she already had experience in the tableware industry. Through an acquaintance from Providence, Francesca Hillyer, who was de Santillana's niece and Venini's granddaughter,[28] Aufiero presented her portfolio and was invited to investigate the production of kiln-fused objects based on her *Mask* sculpture series. In January 1983, she began an eight-week stint at Venini, watching the workers and making test molds; she returned in September and stayed on for a full year. During that time, she set out to build a computer-controlled brick kiln capable of achieving the high temperatures necessary to fuse crushed glass packed in molds, a variation on the *pâte de verre* process and one that de Santillana was willing to explore for potential use by the company. The project was fraught with technical problems, and the firm never produced her cast-glass designs; yet Aufiero continued to make unique objects that she fired in one of the existing kilns. In a more successful endeavor, two of her designs for blown glass, *Alboino* and *Rosamunda*, went into production and remained in the line. Aufiero designed the pieces so workers specializing in mold blowing could make the massive bowls with decorative applications quickly and efficiently.

Aufiero worked in other capacities as needed, including the development of design ideas with de Santillana's daughter, Laura. Aufiero showed the family slides of work by RISD graduate Zynsky, and she in turn was invited to work for Venini at an unspecified future date. An American living in Amsterdam, Zynsky had first traveled to Murano in 1983 to locate materials for her fused-glass sculptures. Early in 1984, she was asked to return to produce a number of unique pieces for a projected series of Venini exhibitions with Aufiero, Carpenter, and Chihuly. Zynsky accepted on the condition that she could bring her small electric kiln and would have the time and space to make her own artwork. She stayed approximately three months; mornings were devoted to sculpture, and afternoons, after the shift was over, were spent working on potential production designs in blown glass with Ongaro, who had an unswerving determination to execute her ideas with precision. Zynsky did not consider herself an industrial designer, and even though she had learned glassblowing at RISD with Dailey, Carpenter, and Chihuly, she credits Ongaro with making her designs truly feasible. Zynsky and Ongaro created vessels with large, turned-lip rims and spun-thread decoration based on the artist's earlier work (plate 55). Under the impression that they were making "warm-ups" for one-of-a-kind pieces, Zynsky sketched the ideas as they worked and used whatever colors were available that day. The de Santillanas considered the experiments a success and put two of them, *Folto* and *Mulinello*, into limited production, where they have remained.

The designs of Zynsky, Aufiero, and Carpenter were included in a 1984 exhibition of historic and contemporary Venini glass held at the Heller Gallery in New York.[29] Despite Aufiero's positive experience at Venini, by the time she departed that same year, she had decided that her future efforts would be applied toward sculpture. After Venini was sold in 1985, the new owners offered Zynsky the position of art director; however, she preferred to make her way as an independent artist.

Each of the American artists had unique goals and experiences, but all realized that their time at Venini was a once-in-a-lifetime opportunity that had a profound impact on their work. Without these experiences, American studio glass would have evolved quite differently. De Santillana's assumption of the leadership position at Venini was perfectly timed with the needs of the developing contemporary glass movement. He opened a window onto the inner workings of Italian glassmaking that was unprecedented, the repercussions of which no one could have anticipated. It's true that international studio glass was being held back by a shortage of technical information and training, and yet, if students had gained exposure to Venini much earlier, they would not have possessed the basic skills needed to appreciate the brilliance of the workers there. The Americans were given the chance to observe and learn glassmaking techniques from some of the finest craftspeople in the world, to study the ways of the industry, and, of equal importance, to experience the culture of Murano and of Venice at large. When that newfound knowledge was disseminated back to the States, it quickly and dramatically raised the standards of craftsmanship. The European team approach definitely changed the way American glassmaking was taught and enhanced the learning process. Rather than struggling to accomplish all the complicated steps alone, students learned more quickly by working in concert with others. And while it is true that eventually the level of craftsmanship would have risen on its own, there is no doubt that without the Venini experiences and the generous vision of a few special individuals, such growth might have taken years, or even generations, longer.

The rewards for Venini, on the other hand, were minimal. Taking on the studio glass artists was something of an altruistic venture that cost the company both time and money; although they were genuinely grateful, the foreign students absorbed the rich experience and then left. Prindle has pointed out that de Santillana was an educator who created what was in essence a teaching situation.[30] The director saw that the Americans had few preconceptions about glass and had the potential to make a contribution to the field. He also knew that they truly appreciated and respected what was laid out before them.[31]

Today, it is not as imperative for American students to seek out such experiences because so much information is readily available to them. Even though the experiment ended in 1985, when the family was separated from Venini, the benefits continue worldwide through the perpetuation of brilliant glassmaking techniques. And although the manner of manipulating the glass may be Italian, in the finest examples, the results are never imitative. In the final analysis, de Santillana, Ongaro, and a few other farsighted members of the Muranese glass community can be credited not only for their contributions to international studio glass but also for helping to preserve Murano's unparalleled heritage.

American Artists at Venini & C.

1950
Kenneth George Scott

1951
Eugene Berman

1955
Charles Lin Tissot

DECEMBER 1960–NOVEMBER 1962
Thomas Stearns

DECEMBER 1968–SPRING 1969
Dale Chihuly

SEPTEMBER 1969–JUNE 1970
Richard Marquis (assisted by Robert Naess, April–June 1970)

OCTOBER 1971–MAY 1972
James Carpenter

JUNE 1972–MAY 1973
Michael Nourot and John Milner

JUNE 1972
Marvin Lipofsky; second visit in June 1975

AUGUST 1972–AUGUST 1973
Dan Dailey

JANUARY 1974–JUNE 1975
William Prindle

SEPTEMBER 1978–MAY 1979, SEPTEMBER 1979–MAY 1980
Benjamin Moore

JANUARY–FEBRUARY 1983, SEPTEMBER 1983–SEPTEMBER 1984
Tina Aufiero

FEBRUARY–APRIL 1984
Toots Zynsky

Notes

I am grateful to the following individuals who agreed to be interviewed for this project: Tina Aufiero, James Carpenter, Dale Chihuly, John Heald Cook, Dan Dailey, Anna Venini Diaz de Santillana, Marvin Lipofsky, Richard Marquis, Benjamin Moore, Michael Nourot, Checco Ongaro, William Prindle, Thomas Stearns, Lino Tagliapietra, and Toots Zynsky. Additional thanks are extended to Kate Elliot of Elliot-Brown Gallery and Heller Gallery for their generous assistance.

1 Slightly different dates for Berman and Scott are cited in Helmut Ricke and Eva Schmitt, *Italian Glass, Murano–Milan, 1930–1970* (Munich: Prestel, 1977), 315. The same source mentions a design executed at Venini by Philadelphia-based Oskar Stonorov.

2 Conversation with the author, October 18, 1995. During his first visit to Venice, Littleton was given less than one hour of hands-on experience with glassblowing on a factory floor before he was escorted from the premises. While visiting Venice in 1967, Littleton's student Audrey Handler gained brief admittance to the Venini factory operations but was unsuccessful in attaining a more lengthy stay.

3 Thomas Stearns, "The Facades of Venice: Recollections of My Residency in Venice, 1960–1962," in *The Venetians: Modern Glass, 1919–1990* (New York: Muriel Karasik Gallery, 1989), 63–68. This essay is a detailed account of Stearns' time at Venini.

4 Conversation with the author, March 18, 1995.

5 This is one side of a debate that continues in Murano to this day.

6 According to Stearns, conversation with the author, March 18, 1995.

7 The *Facades of Venice* were made in three versions, but the first and second exist only as prototypes. They were meant to be displayed in groups of two and three.

8 Only three examples of the *Standing Sentinels* were produced in glass, and they are all different sizes.

9 Though no American artists worked at Venini between 1963 and 1968, an interesting development was taking place elsewhere on Murano. In 1956, the American artist Robert Willson began a series of annual visits to supervise the production of his sculpture designs in molten glass. He hired various glassmakers to collaborate with him, including Fratelli Toso, Alfredo Barbini, and Ars Murano/Ilirichi in 1989. Though he was not a glass craftsman, Willson did assist in the making of his work.

10 Venini & C. was invited to exhibit glass at the first World Congress of Craftsmen, held at Columbia University, New York, in 1964. In a letter of May 3, 1968, to Paul Perrot, de Santillana expressed gratitude for the gift of a catalogue from the first Toledo Glass National, a copy of the newly published *Visual Art in Glass* by Dominick Labino, and a press release from an exhibition of glass sculpture by Andre Billeci at the Corning Museum of Glass. Letter in the files at the Corning Museum of Glass, Corning, New York.

11 Letter from Paul Perrot to Ludovico Diaz de Santillana, September 3, 1968. Letter in the files at the Corning Museum of Glass, Corning, New York.

12 Letter from Anna Venini Diaz de Santillana to the author, November 3, 1995.

13 Letter from Richard Marquis to Anna Venini Diaz de Santillana, March 11, 1995.

14 The word incorporated in Marquis' first word came was *fuck*.

15 Conversation with the author, October 15, 1995.

16 Another studio glass foreigner took up residency during Marquis' stay. The Englishman John Heald Cook had been blowing glass for one year when he graduated from the Royal College of Art in London in 1968. Through an architect acquaintance, he was invited to come to Venini in 1969 as a "visiting designer." Cook arrived with his family in the autumn of 1969 and worked at Venini for three months, departing at the end of the year. After returning to England, he founded the glass program at the University of Leicester, then returned to Venini in January 1970 to work one month more. Cook designed decorative objects that were a combination of vessels and sculpture. None of the designs went into production, and the prototypes were destroyed in the 1972 fire in the Venini administrative offices. To Cook, it seemed that "nothing was impossible at Venini." Conversation with the author, November 2, 1995. The innovations of the firm stood in stark contrast to the rigidity he had experienced at British and Czech factories. A few other American, British, Canadian, and Swedish studio glass artists worked at Venini between 1969 and 1985.

17 Conversation with the author, November 3, 1995.

18 Letter from Ludovico Diaz de Santillana to Paul Perrot, January 11, 1972: "Many regards (?!) by the usual bunch of craft glassmen from USA visiting us, this time Dale Chihuly and Jamie Carpenter—very nice guys, I rather like them and their incredible outofthisworld [sic] love for glass." De Santillana is referring to a visit paid by Chihuly during Carpenter's residence. Letter in the files at the Corning Museum of Glass, Corning, New York.

19 A group of three vessels went briefly into production during Carpenter's first visit. In the late 1970s, his *Calabash*, formed of vertical lengths of spiraling cane, became a commercial success for the company (plate 44).

20 In 1976, Marvin Lipofsky invited Gianni Toso to teach a workshop at the California College of Arts and Crafts in Oakland. Toso gave glassblowing demonstrations over the following years in many American glass departments, including RISD. Toso was the first accomplished Italian glassblower that many American students encountered. He chided the Americans for their lack both of discipline and of respect for the mechanics of the craft, and taught that real art in glass was possible only through the artist's complete control of the material.

21 Useful technical information, especially suitable glass mixture recipes, was difficult for Americans to obtain. In 1971, Nourot was using a formula he found in the *Encyclopedia Britannica*.

22 Conversation with the author, October 26, 1995.

23 Ibid.

24 Prindle believes that the workers were flattered by the photography and didn't mind his documentation because "there is such a big difference between knowing how something is done and being able to do it." Conversation with the author, November 6, 1995.

25 By the late 1970s, increasing numbers of studio glass artists from various countries were making their way to Murano to visit and search for working opportunities. Examples include John Landers, a graduate of the California College of Arts and Crafts, who followed Michael Nourot at Venini, and Rob Adamson, founder of the Glass Eye factory in Seattle, who visited Moore on Murano in 1979.

26 One of Moore's jobs was to pick up refreshments for the workers' breaks. One popular choice was a mixture of half crème de menthe and half anisette. As explained to him by a smiling glassblower, the *taggiata* "makes clean breath for blowing." Moore, conversation with the author, October 25, 1995.

27 During the 1980s, American glassmakers developed studio facilities that could adequately meet the requirements of the visiting Italian teachers. In addition, American skill levels had advanced to such a degree that true assistance could be provided to the Italians in a team situation. Loredano Rosin (with his brother Dino) and Pino Signoretto also became important instructors, particularly of techniques used to form massive, solid sculptures.

28 Francesca's mother, Laura Venini Hillyer, was instrumental in running the company with her father, Paolo Venini, until his death.

29 The exhibition *Venini: The Spirit of the Moment* was organized by Leonard Tomkinson and ran May 5–June 2, 1994. It included Venini objects from the 1950s and 1960s as well as more recent production.

30 Conversation with the author, November 6, 1994.

31 According to Prindle, ibid.

A Conversation with Lino Tagliapietra MATTHEW KANGAS

Lino Tagliapietra working in Seattle, c. 2001.

The following exchange is based on two interviews that took place in Seattle on July 16, 2006, and February 2, 2007. Both interviews were conducted in English. Minor editing has been done for clarity, but nothing substantive has been changed.

Matthew Kangas: What is your earliest memory of glass? How did it all begin?

Lino Tagliapietra: I have two memories of my early life that are very vivid. First, I am playing soccer in the street behind Artisti Vetrai Muranese, and the back door is open. I stop to watch these people; they are yelling and screaming, and then they put something in the annealing oven. I'm very impressed. This is something very big. I don't know exactly what they are doing, but when they are finished, I think, some day, I would like to do something like this.

And second, even before that, when I was a kid—I don't know how old—I remember playing in the factory

where my relatives worked. This is a very confused memory. Yes, I was playing at Venini. They gave me some glass to play with. My mother was sick a lot, so they took me to the factory; it was like a kindergarten for me. And this is the earliest memory of my life.

MK: Before you began your apprenticeship, Italy was ruled by Benito Mussolini and the Fascists. Do you have any memories of that period?

LT: Yes, if I remember correctly, everybody wore the Fascist suit. We saw them as kids. Paolo Venini, for example, I remember seeing him wear the suit. I saw my father and my uncle wear the suit. If they did not, bad things could happen.

MK: Was World War II difficult for you and your family?

LT: It was the low point. I was very young. We were very poor, with very little food. Sometimes we had only

peppers to eat. And there were the ration coupons and the black market. We would take the boat to the countryside and trade glass for salami or corn, to get something to eat. Or for sugar. There was no white sugar. My mother was often very ill and, sometimes, she would say, "No, tonight I am not hungry."

MK: Was there a Fascist aesthetic? I'm thinking, for example, of the works from the 1930s and 1940s that inspired the *Venetians* series (1988–) you made for Chihuly.

LT: No, I don't feel that way, that there was a Fascist style or look. At one point, they did emphasize preserving traditional skills, and we had the big [design] triennales. And we had the patronage from the government. During World War II, we listened in secret to Radio London: "This is Radio London...The moon...is...going...down." That was code for the Normandy [D-Day] landing. We had blackouts for years, and the bombings.

We would hide in our house, in the garden, or behind the big stove. We had a problem to eat, to survive.

MK: Then, after the war, you began your life's work.

LT: Yes. Last summer was the 60th anniversary of my first blowing of glass, on June 16, 1946, at Archimede Seguso's, my first master.

MK: You once told the Japanese art critics Koji Matano and Yoshihiko Takahashi that you began with very small pieces.

LT: Yes, I was eleven. Usually fourteen is too late to start. We worked an incredible amount of time. Even as young kids, we worked from five in the morning to seven at night. And they paid us by the piece. Three people worked on one piece. Six lire per piece I made. For 40 pieces, I'd make 120 lire for my share. The first salary I got, per week, I made 250 lire. I gave everything to my mother and father, of course.

MK: What was Seguso like?

LT: He was a very special person. In our century, [Alfredo] Barbini and Archimede Seguso are the major masters of the 1940–2000 period. Seguso looked skinny and elegant. He worked in a white shirt and had a very soft voice.

When he became angry, everybody knew. One very simple example I'll tell you: With one work, Seguso is watching from far away. It doesn't work right. My master [on the floor, Attilio Frondi] is nervous. So Archimede Seguso comes over. "This is the total opposite of what I want!" Then he says, "Sometimes the smart people are the ones who ask. Proud people are only proud."

And there was another lesson I learned. We were making a vessel and the foot broke. Archimede Seguso says, "Don't throw it away! I'll fix it." He fixed the foot on the spot! He salvaged a broken piece with his fantastic skills.

One more lesson. We tried to make a little rabbit. He says, "I'll show you a different way." And he does it many different ways. He'd start with the foot, and then he'd start the other way. And another way. Each was the same result: the little rabbit. It was perfect, each one.

For me, he was an incredible master because he had a talent for many things.

Oh, I almost forgot to tell you. When Attilio Frondi left, he gave me his tweezers.

MK: So each day you would work very hard.

LT: We have very strange rules there. We start with very unimportant things. [As beginners], we help bring the glass to the annealing oven. Or we bring the water to help cool their hands. We might start with the *pontile* [blowpipe] and then we grow from there. We increase our responsibilities. If you have the right attitude, they use you more. This is how my life as a glassblower began.

One time, when I was thirteen or fourteen, there was a lot of ribbing on a piece. They liked me, so they let me do it. Then they gave me more difficult ones. From Archimede Seguso's, I went on to Gagliano Ferro.

MK: Do you remember Paolo Venini?

LT: Yes, I was a kid. During World War II, he looked very tall, and he came by vaporetto—the private boat was later. My brother and my father and I talked about him a lot.

Paolo Venini was very charismatic. He changed the face of Murano. He employed the top people because they had the special skills he wanted. He was very demanding. He asked for quality—and he got it.

MK: What about his son-in-law, Ludovico Diaz de Santillana, who took over after Venini's death?

LT: Not the same thing with de Santillana. Now Paolo Venini knew how to manage a factory. Ludovico de Santillana was a wonderful person. He spoke English and French, and he knew every American dialect you can think of: Southern, Boston, Brooklyn. He must've been a wonderful teacher.

As for the factory, he did it because he needed to do it, but he wasn't good at it. He had an incredible talent for choosing artists, though.

MK: We've discussed the Fascists; what about the Communists on Murano?

LT: My father was a Communist. My uncle was a Socialist. About my brother [Silvano Tagliapietra, editor and publisher of *La Voce di Murano*], I never knew. During the war, it was not easy. After, they had it easier. Sometimes [the Communists] were good. The first strike [once the Communists had formed and taken over the unions], we wanted to work one hour less per week. We wanted to finish at four, not five, on Saturday. But another time, General Kesselring passed through Venice. They went on strike because he was a [Nazi] war criminal. That was a silly reason for a strike.

MK: And later?

LT: In 1946 and 1948, [Italian Communist Party chair] Togliatti was made minister of justice, but they gave him all the Fascists for his staff! Remember, Matthew, in Italy, we had no Nuremberg trials.

At one point, the Communist Party was bad. Sometimes, they used political power for very stupid exercises only. They wanted a Soviet Union version of everything. They flattened out everything, like the glasshouses, when the unions arrived.

MK: What about Egidio Costantini? He got works by Picasso, Max Ernst, and many others executed in glass. This was good for Venice, wasn't it?

LT: He did not get the same respect as Paolo Venini. He used Murano for his own thing. He acted like a maestro and yet he had no skills. He combined business with art. He would go to the other masters, and they did a wonderful job for him. People complain that the masters were never mentioned by Costantini. "Picasso and Costantini" was how the works were signed.

MK: And how do you rank Barbini?

LT: Unbelievable! He is one of the few examples of skill matched by art. *Massiccio* [solid glass] and blowing! A talented person with an incredible attitude. Around 1936, he worked with Archimede Seguso, but they had a tension and Barbini moved on.

Gino Cenendese was another very important person. He did things very differently than Costantini. All the masters who worked with Cenendese, they became famous. Not so under Costantini.

MK: And Loredano Rosin? His tragically premature death from the Jet Ski accident robbed Venetian glass of another potentially great master.

LT: Yes. He had two passions, women and work. He always said, "When I no longer can have sex, I will continue to work."

MK: What about the future of American and Italian glass?

LT: It will be tough for Murano. I really have no idea; it's too complex. For the U.S., it's quite different. We have a lot of energy. The future may be up and down, but in general I am very hopeful about glass in the U.S. As for Italy, I cannot guess.

Lino Tagliapietra, Italian, b.1934. *Borneo* (detail), 1994, glass, blown, with *zanfirico*; Carnegie Museum of Art

Benjamin Moore, Francesco "Checco" Ongaro, and Rina Ongaro, Venice, 1978.

A Conversation with Benjamin Moore   MATTHEW KANGAS

The following interview took place in Seattle on January 30 and February 13, 2007. Moore's comments are based on his stays at Venini from September 1978 to May 1979 and from September 1979 to May 1980 and on subsequent visits through 2006.

Matthew Kangas: Would you comment briefly on the setup and atmosphere on Murano Island when you arrived there in 1978?

Benjamin Moore: So much of it for me had to do with the timing—when I was there. I got to watch great glassblowers at Venini and also go around to watch others with Louis Sclafani, who was the only other American working in Venice at the time. Louis would come into Venini and watch, and other times he and I would venture out together to Loredano [Rosin]'s studio, or to Barovier and Toso, or to Fratelli Toso. And

we'd watch the great cup maker Caramea, who isn't working any longer.

MK: What does *caramea* mean?

BM: Everybody had a nickname. Carlo Tosi's was Caramea, or caramel or candy. My nickname was Bagalina, or walking stick, because I was so tall and skinny. Checco [Ongaro]'s was Cera, which means wax. Lino [Tagliapietra]'s was Buranello; his family came from the island of Burano originally.

MK: What were some of the differences you noticed between American and Italian working methods?

BM: With such a rich tradition going back to the 10th century, they had certain ways of doing things there. In the States, we were all self-taught. Even when I worked with Marvin [Lipofsky], he'd do a demo and then tell me to just blow glass. It was totally exploratory.

In Italy, they had very strict ways of doing things. Because it was such an intense commercial enterprise, speed was of the utmost importance. We had to make so many pieces per hour, they had to all be a certain way, and so on. These were the polar differences. Everything was new here; there, it was all set.

MK: What was your sense in general of the Italians' attitude toward Venetian glass?

BM: When I was studying Italian in Rome [at the Rhode Island School of Design's Rome program], they really looked down on Venetian glass. They thought it was crap. They knew nothing of [Carlo] Scarpa and [Napoleone] Martinuzzi.

Then, when I was in Venice, everybody was very knowledgeable. When I rented my room in a private home near the Piazza San Marco, the family was very impressed that I was working at Venini. They knew the names of all the big glasshouses.

By the way, in this home, I had to request hot water every time I wanted to bathe or shave!

MK: What was the situation at Venini when you got there? They had been through a tough patch after the death of Paolo Venini in 1959.

BM: Saudi Arabia was keeping Venini afloat. And so was Prince Rainier of Monaco. They commissioned huge architectural lighting fixtures for their palaces. The stuff for Monaco was terrible—octopus-style, giant chandeliers. It seemed as if all the big commissions were coming from the Middle East—and Asia.

MK: What about all the designers that Venini brought in to improve things? Did that have an impact on the other houses?

BM: For one thing, all the other decorative arts and media were not as inbred as glass. It was isolated on this island. And it was a commercial venture always.

This created a kind of ugly situation. The workshops were so stacked up against one another in Venice.

Compared to the high design of Milan in clothing and furniture, the status of glass didn't change until Paolo Venini came on the scene. It was only when the other houses saw how much money and notoriety were possible that they changed—for a while.

MK: What about the whole history of schools for glassblowing opening and closing in Venice? Why haven't they worked out better?

BM: It's due to a combination of things—the set old ways, lots of unconstructive kibitzing, and a lack of leadership. I taught at the latest one, [Scuola di] Abate Zanetti, two summers ago. It's funded by the Commune de Venezia, but the big problem is the provincial attitude of the local glassblowers: for them, there can be only one way to do things. It has to be more open.

And there are a lot of masters who refuse to teach there. All this petty ego stuff. Just the opposite of Pilchuck!

I feel bad for the Venetians because the tradition is so omnipotent.

MK: What would need to happen for things to improve? It seems like a school would be a very important step.

BM: They need some brilliant, open-minded, visionary director who could see to the curriculum change. There are other faculty from around the world who come and bring new ideas, but after they go, then, there's nothing dynamic. There's that isolation of Venice again.

MK: Despite your pessimism, do you see anything bright on the horizon for Venetian glass?

BM: Of course, there's some new exploration, but, for the most part, no, the tradition is so overpowering that it's unlikely that people will approach the materials in a fresh fashion. Mostly, they're just rehashing old stuff. And one of the curses of glassmaking is the high overhead. With all these expenses, you have to make a product. But Simone Cenendese is a possibility. He's a very talented young man. Andrea Zilio's another. And Cesare Toffolo.

MK: Are there any very young people going into the factories, as Lino and Checco did?

BM: There are very few young people in the factories, and yet there are more than when I was there. The number of glasshouses has become small; it's dwindling. Lino and Checco did not encourage their sons to go into the glass factories. They became translators or accountants instead.

MK: Could you summarize what you think are the causes of the decline of Italian glass in recent decades?

BM: You can't say there was just one thing. First, there was the tradition; it stifled creativity. Second, there was a generalized loss of appreciation for handmade glass tableware. Next, there was the Communist takeover of the unions in Italy. All salaries were equalized, regardless of skill levels. That drove dozens of the workers away. Also, there wasn't the Scandinavian model where the country's best artists were invited to work there. Venini did that, but he was the only one. And, finally, as the general economic level became higher in Italy, fewer people wanted to go into glass.

Benjamin Moore, American, b. 1952; *Palla Set* (detail), 1994, glass, blown; Carnegie Museum of Art

VivaVetro! GlassAlive! VENICE AND AMERICA

The Italian Legacy

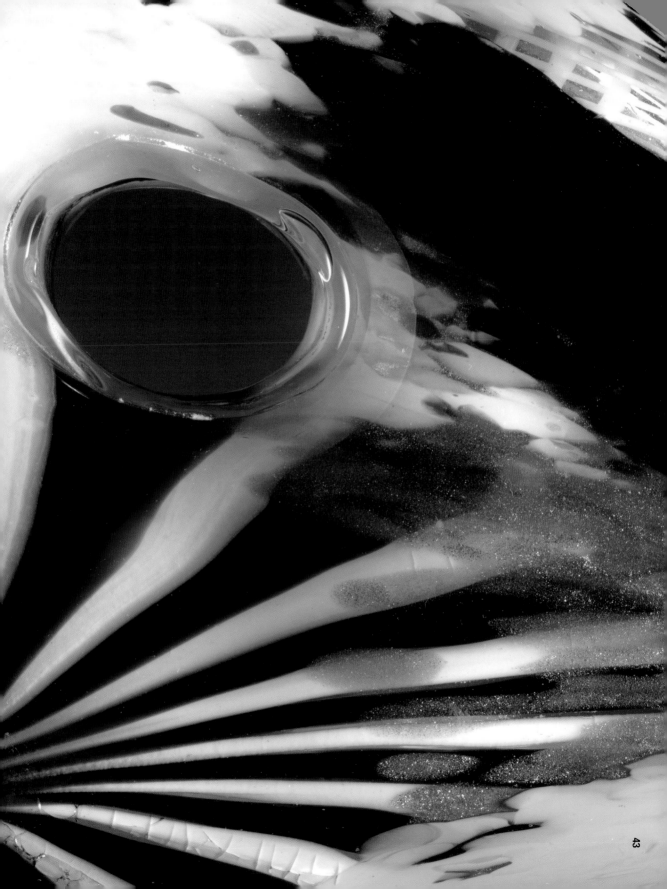

PLATE 1 **ALFREDO BARBINI**
Biennale Vase, 1962, 10 x 8 1/2 x 4 1/2 in. (25.40 x 21.60 x 11.40 cm)

PLATE 2 **NICOLÒ BAROVIER**
Large Vase with Inflated Murrine, c. 1914,
18 15/16 x diam. 10 in. (48.10 x diam. 25.40 cm)

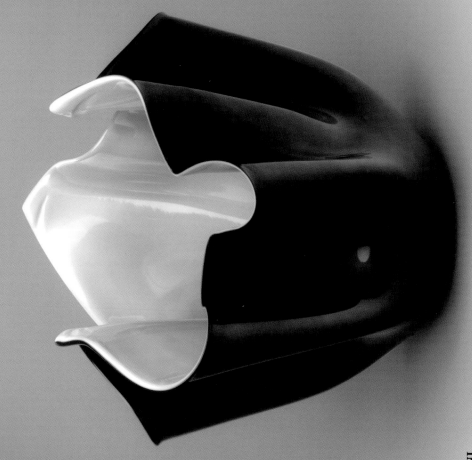

46

PLATE 3 **FULVIO BIANCONI**
Fazzoletto Vase, designed 1949, 10 1/4 x diam. 11 1/2 in.
(26.04 x diam. 29.21 cm)

PLATE 4 **FULVIO BIANCONI**

Fasce Orizzontali Vase, 1953–1954. 12 x diam. 11 1/16 in.
(30.50 x diam. 28.10 cm)

PLATE 5 **LAURA DE SANTILLANA**
Numeri Plate, 1977, 1 3/8 x diam. 10 3/4 in. (3.49 x diam. 27.30 cm)

PLATE 6 **ANZOLO FUGA**
Dish, c. 1956, 5 x 19 x 17 in.
(12.70 x 48.30 x 43.20 cm)

PLATE 7 **DINO MARTENS**
Bottiglia Allegria, designed 1952, 24 x diam. 4 9/16 in.
(61 x diam. 11.59 cm)

PLATE 8 **DINO MARTENS**
Oriente Vase, 1954, 15 1/2 x 7 x 4 in.
(39.37 x 17.80 x 10.20 cm)

PLATE 9 **NAPOLEONE MARTINUZZI**
Black Cactus, 1928–1930, 13 1/2 x diam. 3 11/16 in.
(34.29 x diam. 9.37 cm)

PLATE 10
NAPOLEONE MARTINUZZI
Amphora, 1930, 12 7/8 x 13 1/4 x 10 in.
(32.70 x 33.66 x 25.40 cm)

54

PLATE 11 **GIULIO RADI**
Reazioni Policrome, c. 1947–1952, 14 1/4 x 4 1/2 x 4 1/8 in.
(36.20 x 11.43 x 10.48 cm)

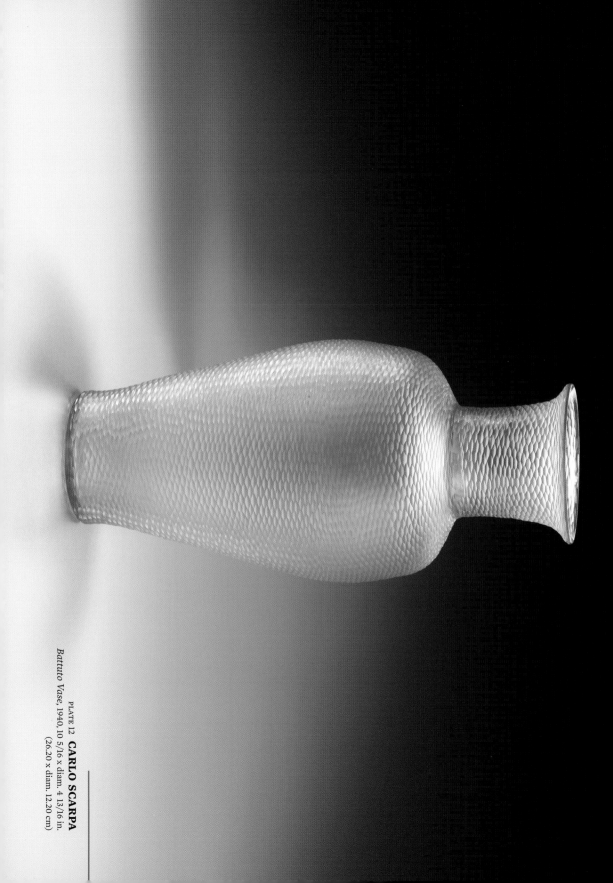

PLATE 12 **CARLO SCARPA**

Battuto Vase, 1940, 10 5/16 x diam. 4 13/16 in.
(26.20 x diam. 12.20 cm)

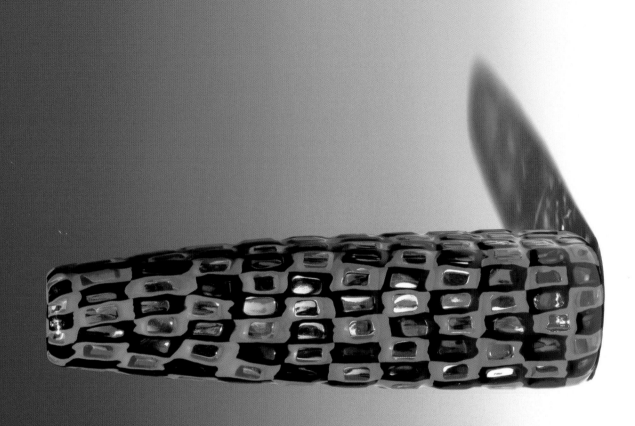

PLATE 13 **TOBIA SCARPA**
Occhi Vase, designed 1959–1960, 12 1/2 x 3 5/16 x 3 1/4 in.
(31.80 x 8.70 x 8.40 cm)

PLATE 14 **ARCHIMEDE SEGUSO**

A *Merletto Vase*, 1953, 9 3/4 x diam. 7 7/16 in.
(24.70 x diam. 18.90 cm)

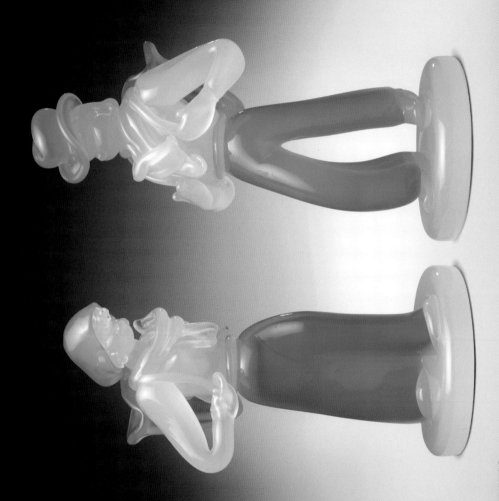

PLATE 15 **ARCHIMEDE SEGUSO**
Two Peasants, 1959, 11 x diam. 5 in. (27.90 x diam. 12.70 cm),
9 3/4 x diam. 5 in. (24.80 x diam. 12.70 cm)

PLATE 16 **VITTORIO ZECCHIN**

Veronese Vase, designed 1921, 10 9/16 x diam. 5 13/16 in. (26.83 x diam. 14.76 cm)

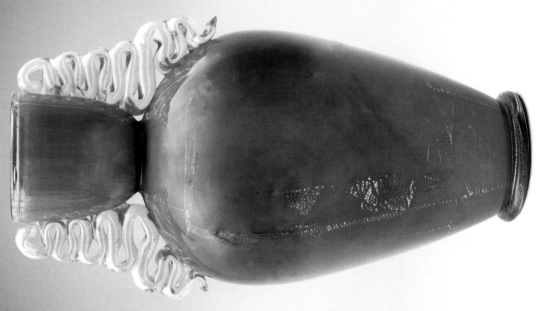

PLATE 17 **FRANCESCO ZECCHIN**
AND NAPOLEONE MARTINUZZI
Large Velato with Curly Handles, c. 1932, 16 7/8 x 7 3/4 x 8 1/2 in.
(42.86 x 19.68 x 21.59 cm)

PLATE 18 **TONI ZUCCHERI**
Scolpito Vase, 1967, 13 7/16 x diam. 3 in.
(34.20 x diam. 7.75 cm)

PLATE 19 **TONI ZUCCHERI**
Tronchi Vase, 1967, 13 x diam. 2 3/4 in.
(33 x diam. 7 cm)

American Designers

PLATE 20 **EUGENE BERMAN**
Obelisk with Masks, 1951, 12 13/16 x 3 1/4 x 3 3/16 in.
(32.60 x 8.20 x 8 cm)

PLATE 21 **EUGENE BERMAN**
Vase in Form of a Well Head, 1951,
5 3/4 x diam. 6 1/2 in. (14.61 x diam. 16.51 cm)

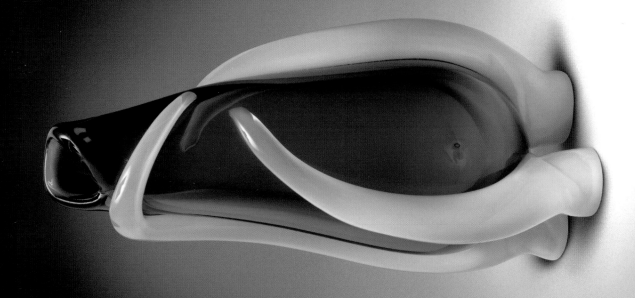

PLATE 22 **CLAIRE FALKENSTEIN**
Blue and White Vase, 1972–1973, 17 1/8 x 8 1/4 x 7 in.
(43.50 x 20.95 x 17.80 cm)

PLATE 23 **CLAIRE FALKENSTEIN**
Bottle-Necked Vase with 2 Rings, c. 1972.
9 9/16 x 6 3/16 x 3 15/16 in. (24.30 x 15.70 x 10.10 cm)

PLATE 24   **KENNETH GEORGE SCOTT**
Three Fish and a Snail, 1950–1970, 3 x 6 1/4 in. (7.60 x 15.90 cm), 3 x 12 1/2 in.
(7.60 x 31.80 cm), 2 1/2 x 5 3/4 in. (6.40 x 14.60 cm), 2 1/2 x 3 15/16 in. (10 x 6.40 cm)

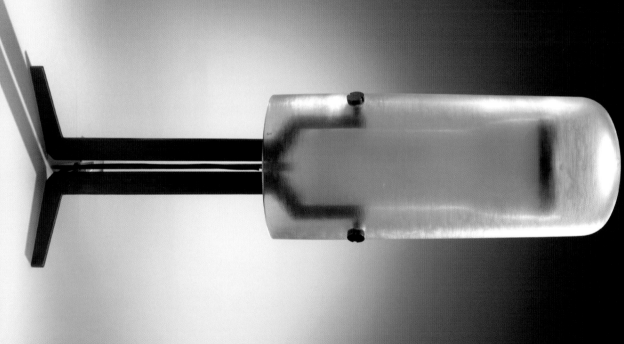

PLATE 25 **THOMAS STEARNS**
Doge Desk Lamp for Signing Decrees, c. 1961,
26 x diam. 9 in. (66 x diam. 22.90 cm)

PLATE 26 **THOMAS STEARNS**
Cappello del Doge, 1961–1962,
5 7/8 x diam. 5 3/8 in. (14.90 x diam. 13.70 cm)

PLATE 27 **THOMAS STEARNS**
Facades of Venice, 1962,
15 1/2 x 3 1/2 x 2 in. (39.37 x 8.89 x 5.10 cm),
16 1/2 x 4 3/4 x 2 3/4 in. (41.91 x 12.07 x 6.99 cm)

PLATE 28 **CHARLES LIN TISSOT**
Chess Set, 1955, 5 3/8 x 22 x 22 in. (13.65 x 55.90 x 55.90 cm)

PLATE 29   **CHARLES LIN TISSOT**
Birdcage, 1959,
26 3/4 x 24 x 23 1/4 in. (67.95 x 61 x 59.05 cm)

PLATE 30 **CHARLES LIN TISSOT**
Cypress Tree Centerpiece, 1961, 13 3/8 x diam. 20 3/4 in.
(34 x diam. 52.60 cm)

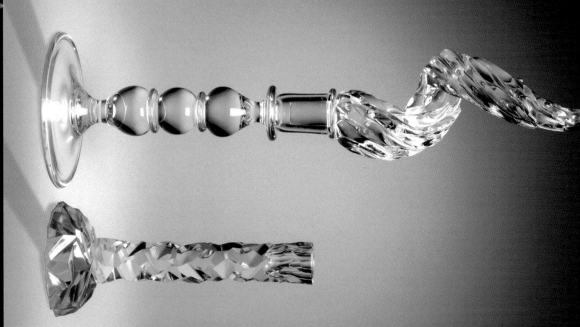

PLATE 31 **CHARLES LIN TISSOT**
Faceted Candlestick, 1964, 10 1/2 x diam. 4 1/2 in.
(26.67 x diam. 11.43 cm);
Flame Candlestick, 1964, 23 1/2 x diam. 6 1/4 in.
(59.69 x diam. 15.88 cm)

Robert Willson

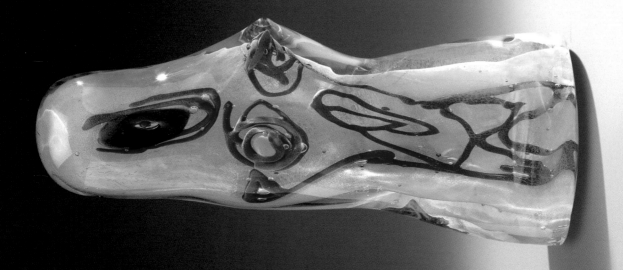

PLATE 32 **ROBERT WILLSON**
Mirage Myth, 1970, 16 x 6 1/2 x 5 in.
(40.60 x 16.51 x 12.70 cm)

PLATE 33 **ROBERT WILLSON**
Texas Longhorn, c. 1983,
16 1/4 x 11 5/8 x 5 3/4 in. (41.28 x 29.46 x 14.61 cm)

PLATE 34 **ROBERT WILLSON**
Red Nile (People), 1991, 26 x 12 x 6 in.
(66 x 30.50 x 15.20 cm)

La Fucina degli Angeli

PLATE 35 **JEAN ARP**
Nude, 1964, 10 1/8 x 5 x 13 3/8 in. (25.72 x 12.70 x 33.97 cm)

PLATE 36 **MAX ERNST**
Bird, 1964, 15 1/8 x 8 3/4 x 3 1/4 in.
(38.42 x 22.22 x 8.26 cm)

PLATE 37 **SHANE GUFFOGG**
Return the Find, 2005, 12 x 7 x 8 in. (30.50 x 17.80 x 20.30 cm)

PLATE 38   **PAUL JENKINS**
Phenomena One Pole of the Twelve Pole Creek,
1969, 20 1/8 x 6 1/2 x 3 1/2 in. (51.12 x 16.51 x 8.89 cm)

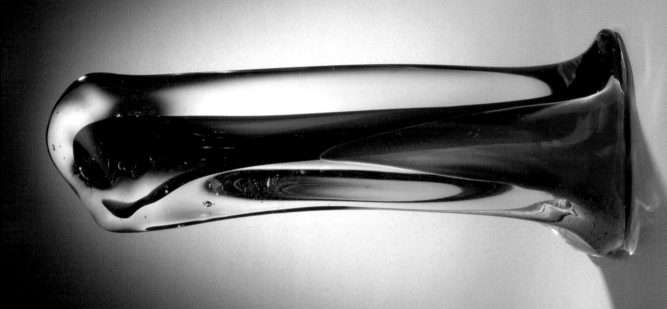

PLATE 39 **PAUL JENKINS**
Phenomena Blue Stele, 1970, 23 x 10 x 7 in.
(58.40 x 25.40 x 17.80 cm) overall

PLATE 40   **PAUL JENKINS**
Phenomena Chalice Fold, 1970, 15 1/2 x 7 x 5 1/2 in.
(39.37 x 17.80 x 13.97 cm)

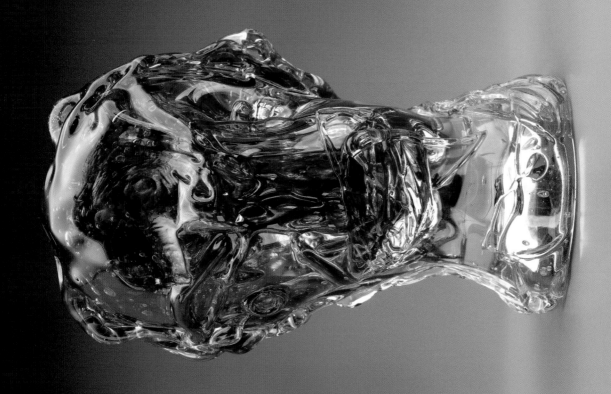

PLATE 41 **MARK TOBEY**
Visage, 1966, 18 in. (45.70 cm) high

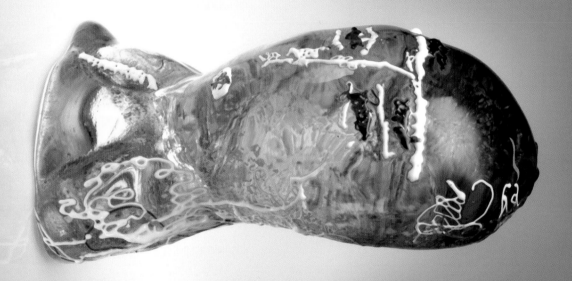

PLATE 42 **MARK TOBEY**

Volto, 1974, 15 x 8 1/4 x 7 1/4 in. (38.10 x 21 x 18.40 cm)

Americans in Venice

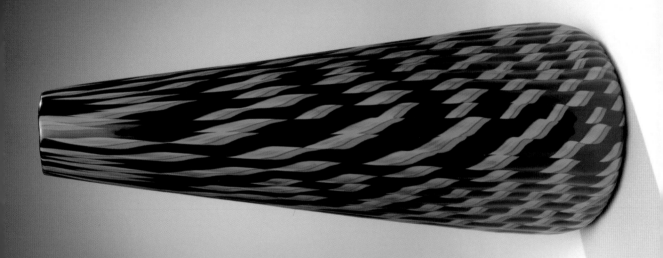

PLATE 43 **JAMES CARPENTER**
Calabash, 1983, 11 1/2 x 4 1/2 x 4 1/8 in.
(29.21 x 11.40 x 10.50 cm)

PLATE 44 **JAMES CARPENTER**
Zebra Vase, 1985, 7 1/2 x 4 5/16 x 7 1/16 in.
(19.10 x 11 x 17.90 cm)

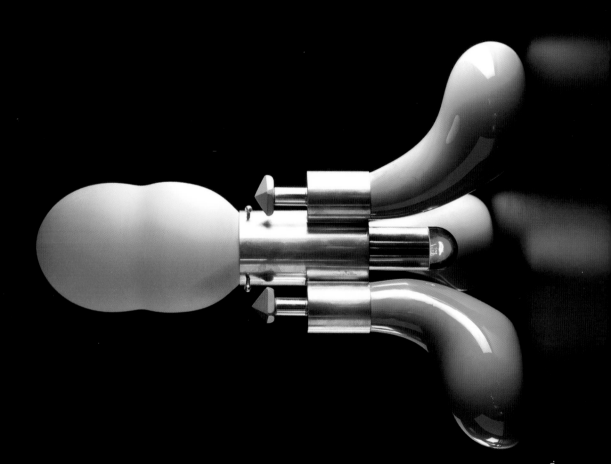

PLATE 45 **DAN DAILEY**
Pistachio Lamp, 1972, 15 1/2 x 11 x 11 in.
(39.40 x 27.90 x 27.90 cm)

PLATE 46 **DAN DAILEY**
Saturn Rocket Lamp, 1972, 10 x 9 x 9 in.
(25.40 x 22.90 x 22.90 cm)

PLATE 47 **MARVIN LIPOFSKY**
Venini Series 1972 #7, 1972, 8 1/2 x 12 x 10 in. (21.59 x 30.50 x 25.40 cm)

PLATE 48 **MARVIN LIPOFSKY**
Fratelli-Toso Series, Split Piece, 1977-1978,
14 x 16 x 18 in. (35.60 x 40.60 x 45.70 cm),
7 x 13 x 10 in. (17.80 x 33 x 25.40 cm)

PLATE 49 **RICHARD MARQUIS**
(right) *Striped Cup,* 1969, 2 1/2 x 4 1/4 x 4 1/4 in. (6.35 x 10.79 x 10.79 cm);
(left) *Iridescent Cup,* 1968, 2 1/2 x 5 1/2 x 5 in. (6.35 x 13.97 x 12.70)

PLATE 50 **RICHARD MARQUIS**

American Acid Capsule with Cloth Container, 1969–1970, 4 x diam. 1 1/4 in.
(10.20 x diam. 3.17 cm)

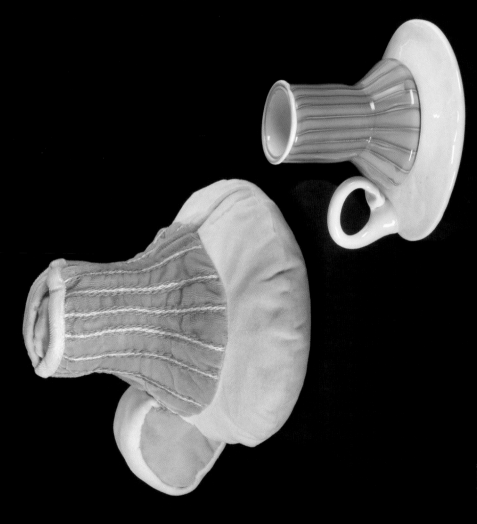

PLATE 51 **RICHARD MARQUIS**
Mae West Cup and Cover, 1969–1970, 3 3/16 x diam. 4 7/16 in.
(8.10 x diam. 11.25 cm)

PLATE 52   **RICHARD MARQUIS**
Red Riding Hood's Grandma's House Landscape Bottles, 1970,
5 1/2 x 4 3/4 x 3 in. (13.97 x 12.07 x 7.60 cm),
4 1/4 x 3 1/2 x 1 3/4 in. (10.79 x 8.89 x 4.45 cm)

PLATE 53 **RICHARD MARQUIS**
Stars and Stripes Cup with Container (Free Speech Cup), 1970,
3 1/2 x 5 1/4 x 4 in. (8.89 x 13.34 x 10.20 cm)

PLATE 54 **WILLIAM PRINDLE**
Cloud Lamp, 1974, 14 x 17 x 14 in. (35.60 x 43.20 x 35.60 cm)

PLATE 55 **TOOTS ZYNSKY**
Chiacchiera, 1984,
13 x diam. 7 in. (33 x diam. 17.80 cm),
10 1/2 x diam. 7 in. (26.67 x diam. 17.80 cm)

Chihuly and Venice

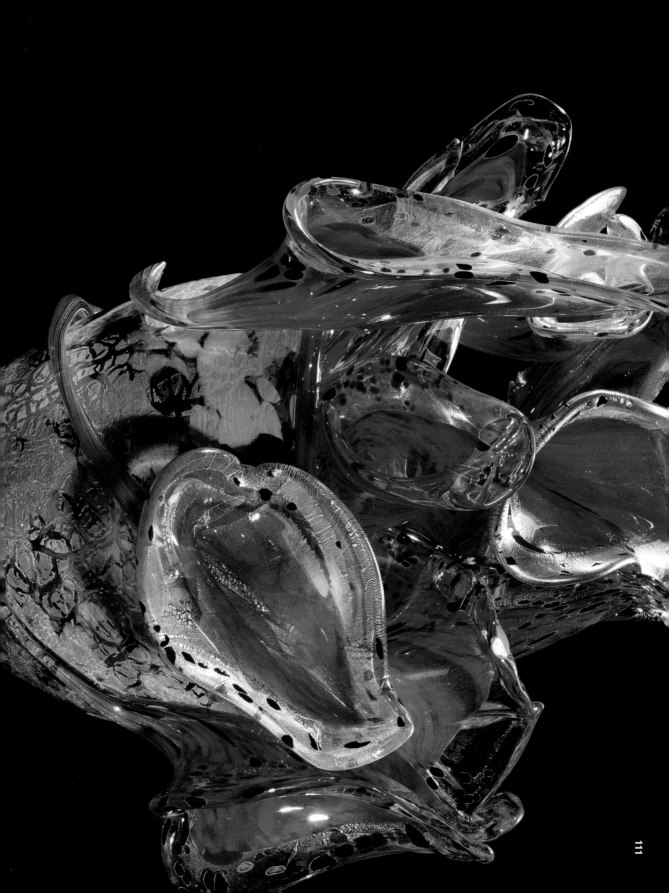

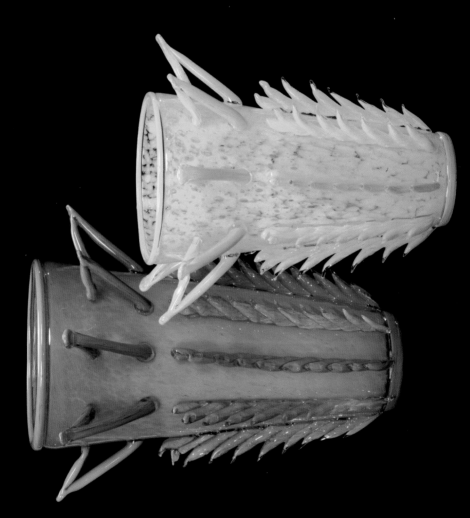

PLATE 56 **DALE CHIHULY**
Olive Green and Chrome Yellow Venetians with Saw-Tooth Flanges, 1988,
17 3/4 x diam. 9 1/16 in. (45.10 x diam. 23 cm), 13 1/8 x diam. 7 1/2 in. (33.50 x diam. 19 cm)

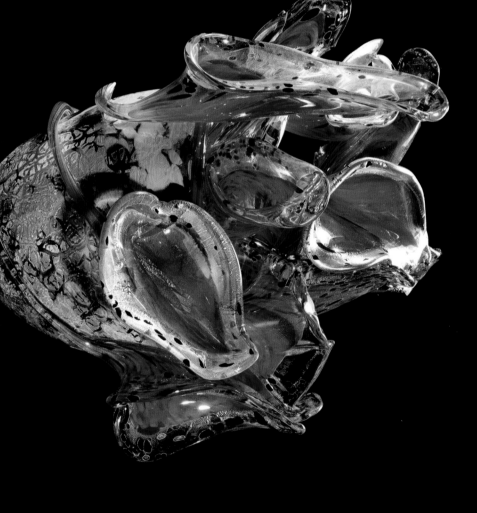

PLATE 57 **DALE CHIHULY**
Cadmium Yellow Venetian with Red Lilies, 1989,
19 x 14 x 16 in. (48.30 x 35.60 x 40.60 cm)

PLATE 58 **DALE CHIHULY**
Cobalt Blue Venetian #410, 1990, 33 x 14 x 11 in.
(83.80 x 35.60 x 27.90 cm)

PLATE 59 **DALE CHIHULY**
Red Spotted Ikebana with Chartreuse Stems, 1992,
44 1/2 x 32 1/2 x 17 in. (113.03 x 82.55 x 43.20 cm)

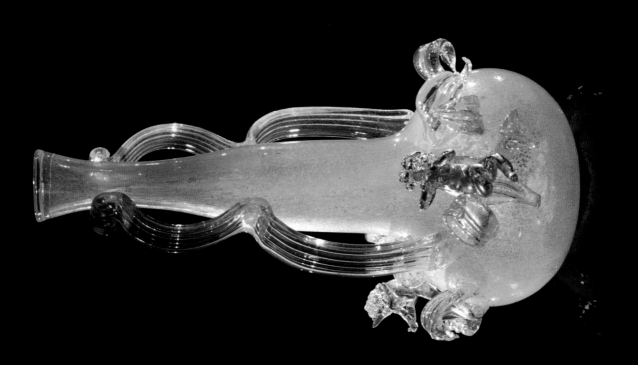

PLATE 60 **DALE CHIHULY**
Cadmium Yellow Putti Venetian, 1993,
27 x 17 x 17 in. (68.60 x 43.20 x 43.20 cm)

PLATE 61   **DALE CHIHULY**
Spotted Raspberry Putti Venetian with Devil on Sunflower,
1994, 19 x 16 x 14 in. (48.30 x 40.60 x 35.60 cm)

Chandeliers and Light

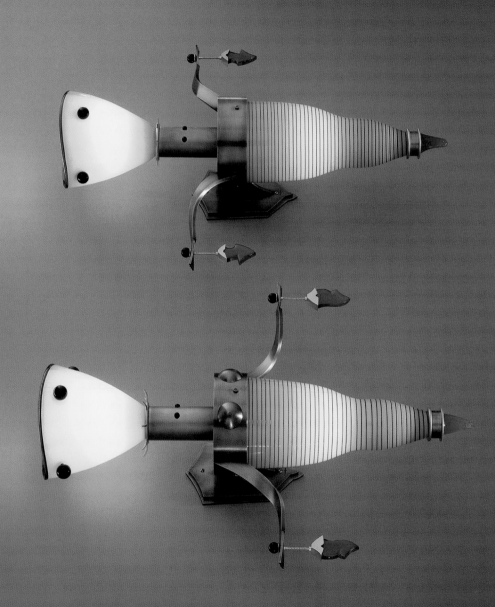

PLATE 62 **DAN DAILEY**
Splendid, 2005, 26 1/2 x 20 1/2 x 8 1/2 in. (67.30 x 52.10 x 21.60 cm)

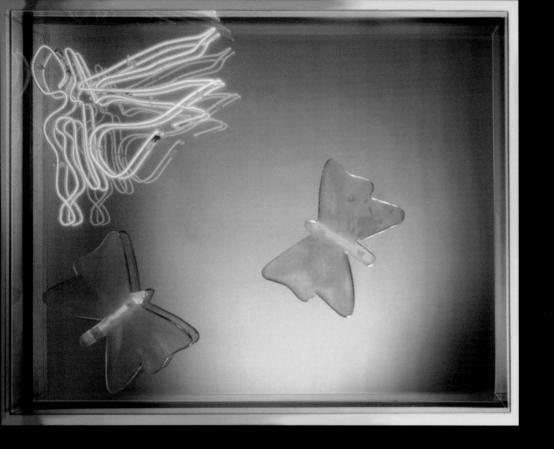

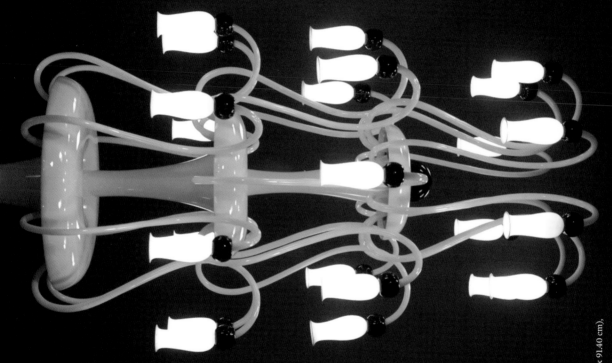

PLATE 64 **JAMES MONGRAIN**
Chandelier, 2005, 70 x 36 x 36 in. (177.80 x 91.40 x 91.40 cm),
exhibited in *Well-Hung: Chandeliers Revealed*,
Pittsburgh Glass Center, 2005

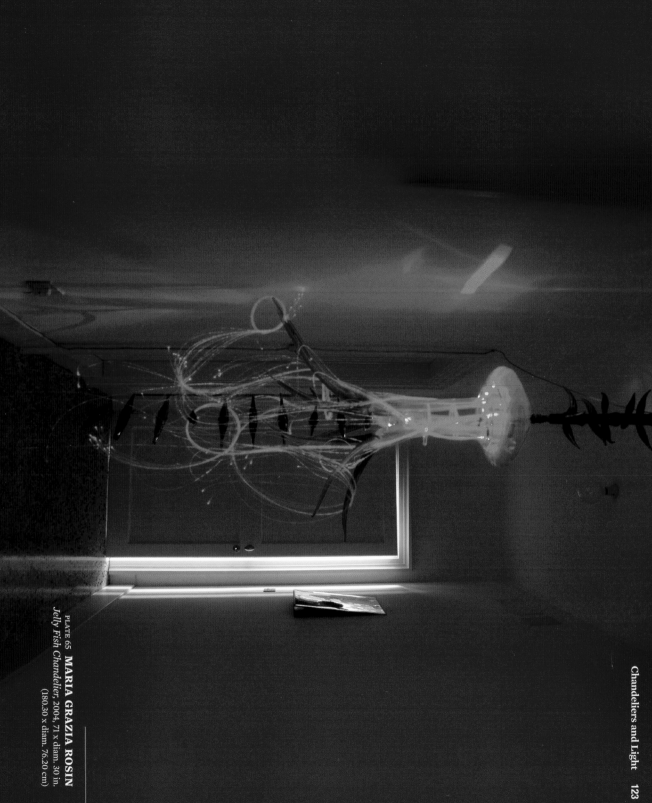

PLATE 65 **MARIA GRAZIA ROSIN**
Jelly Fish Chandelier, 2004, 71 x diam. 30 in.
(180.30 x diam. 76.20 cm)

PLATE 66 **GINNY RUFFNER**
Chandelier, 1989, 39 3/4 x diam. 34 1/4 in.
(100.97 x diam. 87 cm)

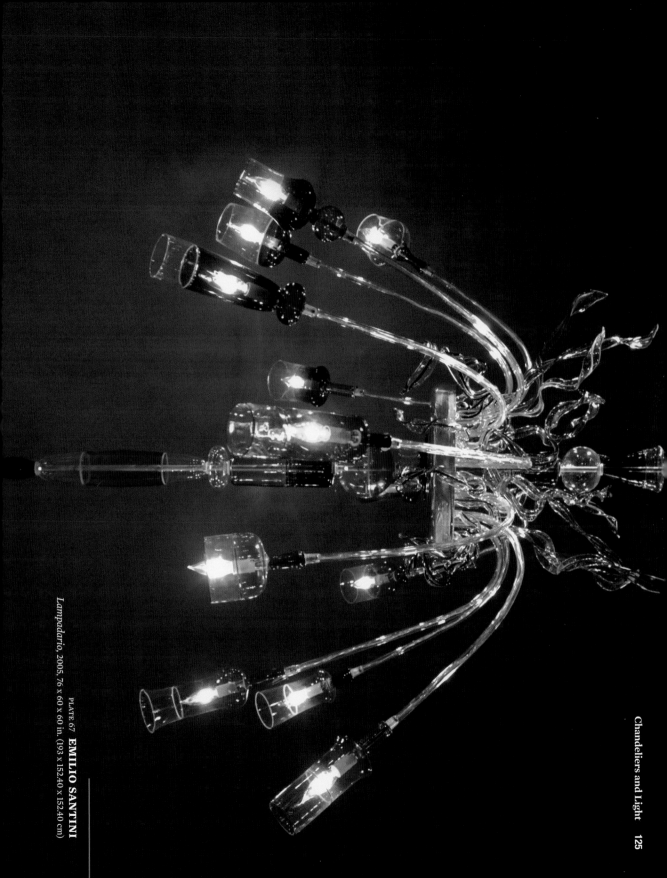

PLATE 67 **EMILIO SANTINI**

Lampadario, 2005, 76 x 60 x 60 in. (193 x 152.40 x 152.40 cm)

Italians in America

PLATE 68 **FEDERICA MARANGONI**
Ciaobella Nikes, designed 1984, 4 5/16 x 11 7/16 x 3 9/16 in. (10.95 x 28.97 x 9.05 cm) each

PLATE 69 **ALESSANDRO MORETTI**

Dish in Tuning Color, 1969, 8 3/4 x diam. 20 1/2 in. (22.20 x diam. 52.10 cm) overall

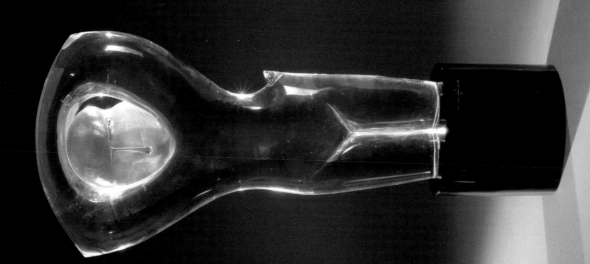

PLATE 70 **LOREDANO ROSIN**
Abstract Standing Figure, c. 1970, 26 x 10 x 4 1/2 in.
(66 x 25.40 x 11.43 cm)

PLATE 71 **LOREDANO ROSIN**

Two Torsos, 1979, 26 x 13 x 7 1/2 in. (66 x 33 x 19.05 cm)

PLATE 72 **LINO TAGLIAPIETRA**
Giano, 1992, 13 3/4 x diam. 6 3/16 in. (34.93 x diam. 15.72 cm)

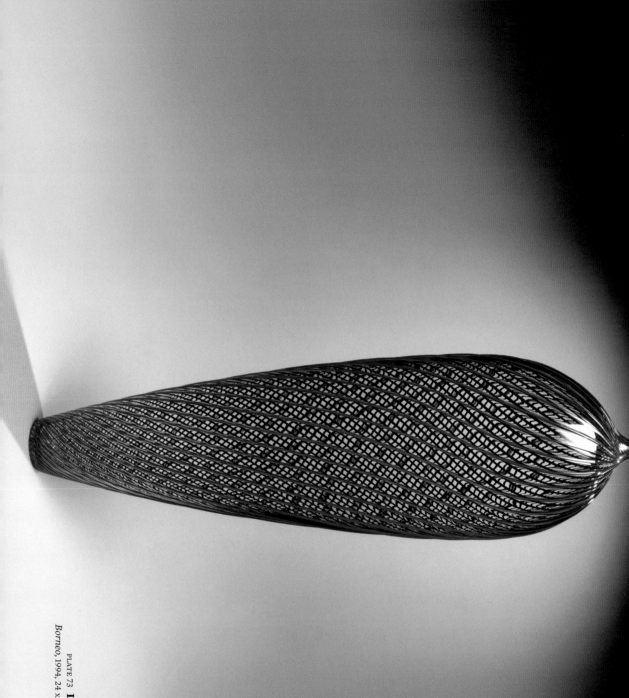

PLATE 73 **LINO TAGLIAPIETRA**
Borneo, 1994, 24 x 7 x 5 in. (61 x 17.80 x 12.70 cm)

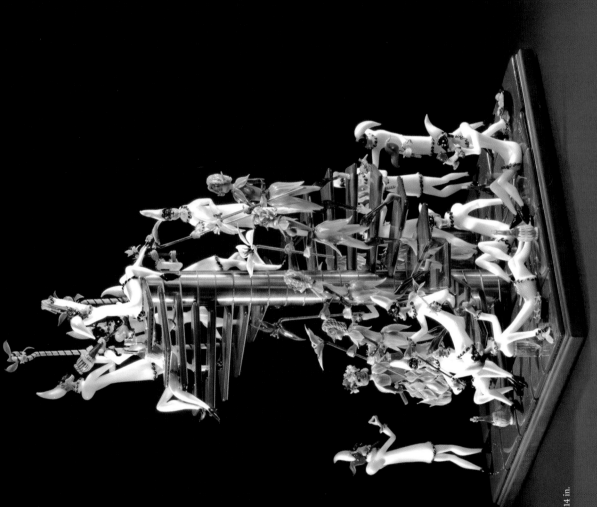

PLATE 74 GIANNI TOSO
Rites of Springtime, 2006, 22 x 14 x 14 in.
(55.90 x 35.60 x 35.60 cm)

Venetian Techniques

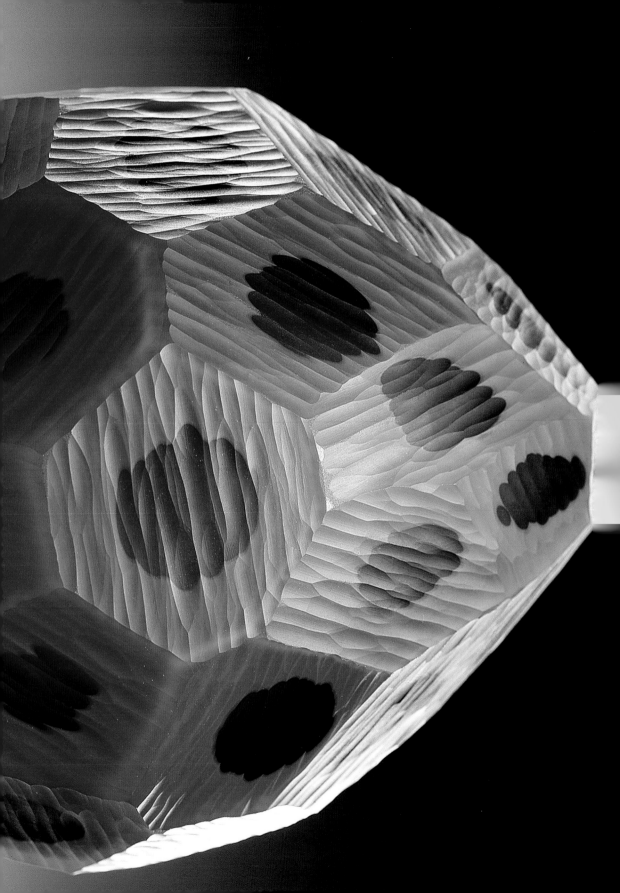

Battuto

PLATE 75 **PHILIP BALDWIN
AND MONICA GUGGISBERG**
Blue + Red Spin, 1997, 21 1/4 x diam. 5 1/2 in.
(53.98 x diam. 13.97 cm)

PLATE 76 **PHILIP BALDWIN
AND MONICA GUGGISBERG**
Faceted Platns in Red, 2001, 10 x diam. 7 7/8 in.
(25.40 x diam. 20 cm)

PLATE 77 **CARLO SCARPA**
Battuto Vase, 1940, 7 7/8 x diam. 6 3/4 in.
(20 x diam. 17.10 cm)

Color and Design

PLATE 78 **FULVIO BIANCONI**
Sasso Vase, 1966–1970, 5 3/4 x diam. 5 3/8 in.
(14.60 x diam. 13.60 cm)

PLATE 79 **FULVIO BIANCONI**
Sasso Vase, 1966–1970, 4 1/2 x 4 9/16 x 3 1/4 in.
(11.50 x 11.60 x 8.20 cm)

PLATE 80 **MARVIN LIPOFSKY**
The Four Seasons—I Quattro Stagioni, Venezia Aperto Vetro, 1998:
Winter—Inverno, 17 x 17 1/2 x 16 1/2 in. (43.18 x 44.45 x 41.91 cm);
Spring—Primavera, 5 x 34 x 5 in. (12.70 x 86.36 x 12.70 cm);
Autumn—Autunno, 12 1/2 x 26 x 13 in. (31.75 x 66.04 x 33.02 cm);
Summer—Estate, 12 x 18 x 14 1/2 in. (30.48 x 45.72 x 36.83 cm)

PLATE 81 **BENJAMIN MOORE**
Palla Set, 1994, 4 1/4 x diam. 18 3/4 in. (10.79 x diam. 47.63 cm),
16 x diam. 5 in. (40.60 x diam. 12.70 cm)

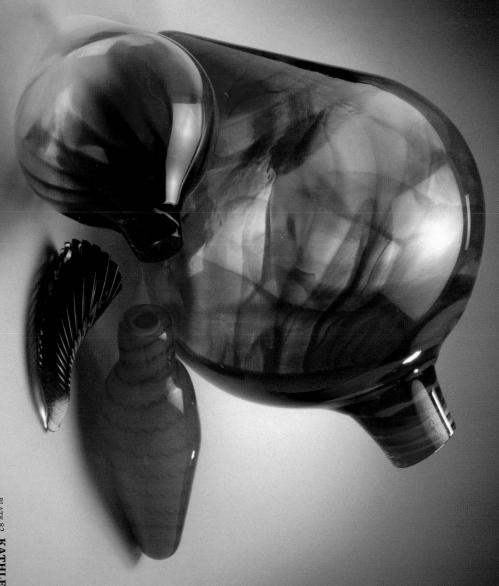

PLATE 82 **KATHLEEN MULCAHY**
In the Fire: Spinner Group in Red, 1992.
8 1/2 x 8 x 10 in. (21.59 x 20.32 x 25.40 cm) ; 3 1/2 x 3 1/4 x 8 in. (8.89 x 8.26 x 20.32 cm) ;
16 x 15 1/2 x 22 in. (40.64 x 39.37 x 55.88 cm), 26 x 5 1/4 x 9 in. (66.04 x 13.34 x 22.86 cm)

PLATE 83 **TOOTS ZYNSKY**
Parapiglia, 2000, 11 x 23 1/2 x 12 1/2 in. (28 x 60 x 32 cm)

Incalmo

PLATE 84 **SONJA BLOMDAHL**
Fuchsia/Violet, 1994, 17 5/8 x diam. 11 5/8 in.
(44.77 x diam. 29.53 cm)

PLATE 85 **NADÈGE DESGENÉTEZ**
Chaussette (dark purple), 2004, 24 1/2 x 8 3/4 x 4 1/2 in.
(62.23 x 22.22 x 11.43 cm)

PLATE 86 **GIO PONTI**
Bottiglie Morandiane, c. 1948-1952,
13 x diam. 4 1/2 in. (33 x diam. 11.43 cm)

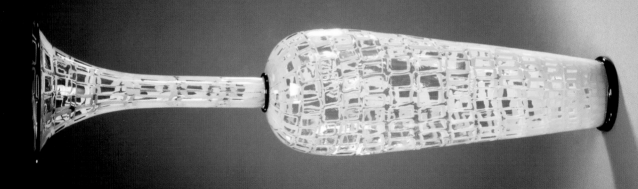

Murrine

PLATE 88 **RICHARD MARQUIS**
Marquiscarpa #19, 1991, 5 1/4 x 7 5/16 x 4 in.
(13.34 x 18.57 x 10.16 cm)

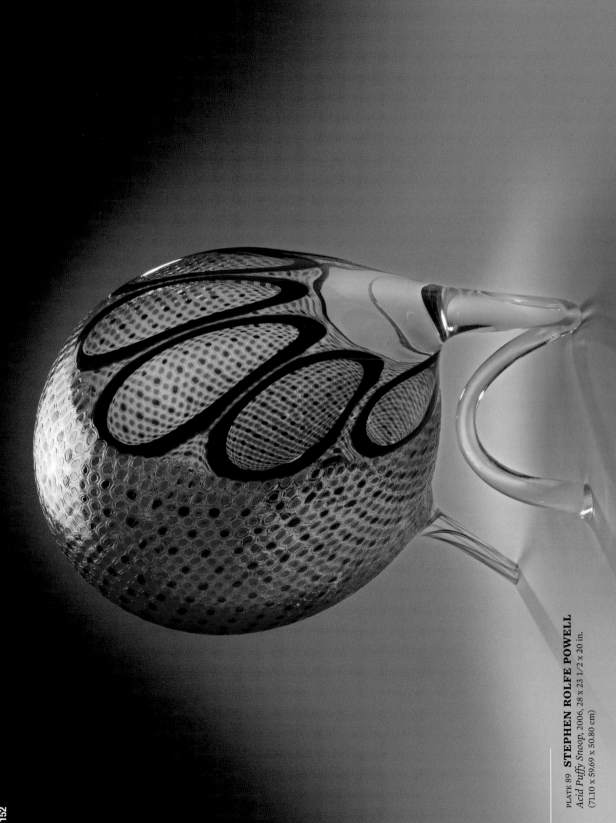

PLATE 89 **STEPHEN ROLFE POWELL**
Acid Puffy Snoop, 2006, 28 x 23 1/2 x 20 in.
(71.10 x 59.69 x 50.80 cm)

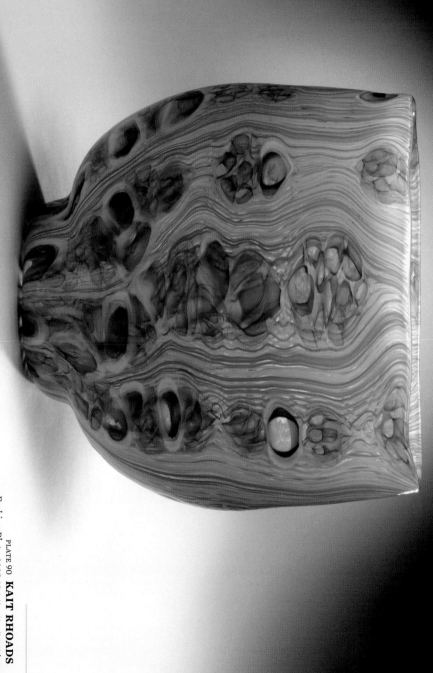

PLATE 90 **KAIT RHOADS**
Fashion Plate, 2005, 10 1/2 x 11 x 7 1/2 in.
(26.67 x 27.90 x 19.05 cm)

PLATE 91 **CARLO SCARPA**
Murrine Plate, c. 1940, 2 1/4 x diam. 10 1/2 in. (5.71 x diam. 26.67 cm)

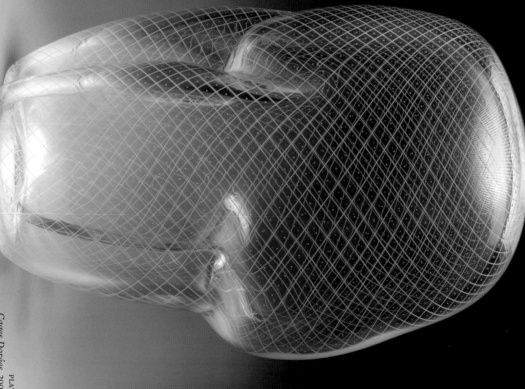

Reticello

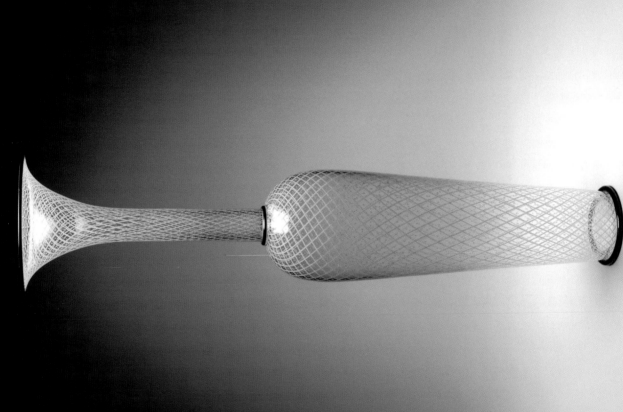

PLATE 93 **DANTE MARIONI**
Reticello Vase, 2001, 26 3/4 x diam. 5 7/8 in.
(67.95 x diam. 14.92 cm)

PLATE 94 ATTRIBUTED TO **SALVIATI & C.**
Platter, 1890s, 2 1/4 x diam. 22 in. (5.71 x diam. 55.90 cm)

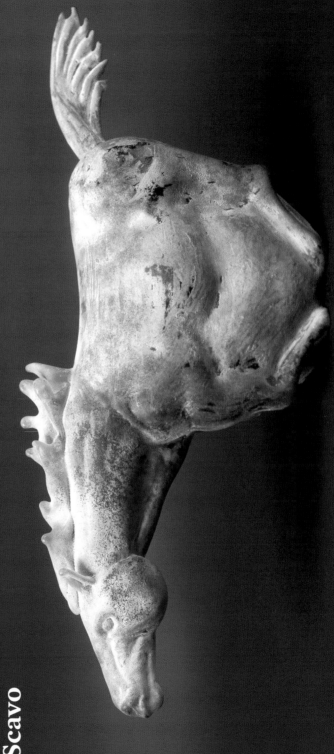

Scavo

PLATE 95 **ALFREDO BARBINI**
Horse, 1959-1960, 10 1/4 x 23 1/2 x 4 in. (26.04 x 59.69 x 10.20 cm)

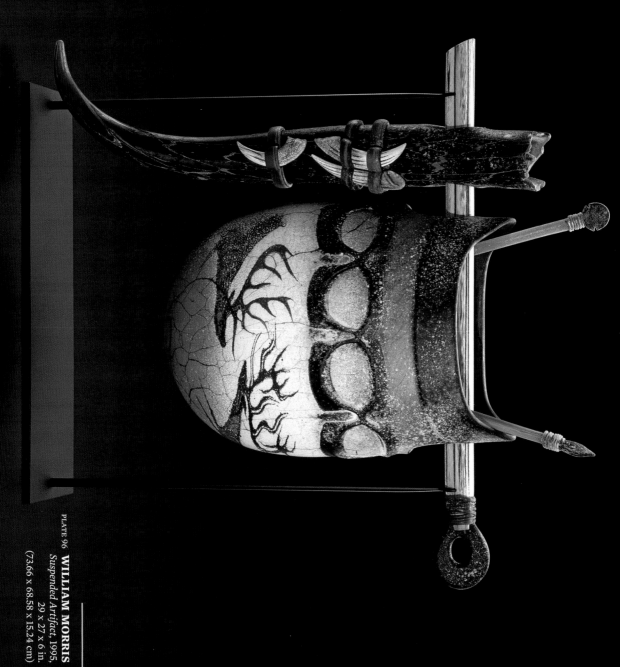

PLATE 96 **WILLIAM MORRIS**
Suspended Artifact, 1995.
29 x 27 x 6 in.
(73.66 x 68.58 x 15.24 cm)

PLATE 97 **WILLIAM MORRIS**
Bird Rattle, 1998, 16 1/8 x 5 x 13 1/2 in.
(40.96 x 12.70 x 34.29 cm)

PLATE 98 **WILLIAM MORRIS**
Rhyton Bull, 1998, 10 1/2 x 7 3/8 x 13 1/2 in.
(26.70 x 18.70 x 34.30 cm)

Tesserae

PLATE 99 **FULVIO BIANCONI**
Pezzato Vase, 1950, 14 11/16 x 5 7/16 x 4 1/16 in.
(37.30 x 13.80 x 10.30 cm)

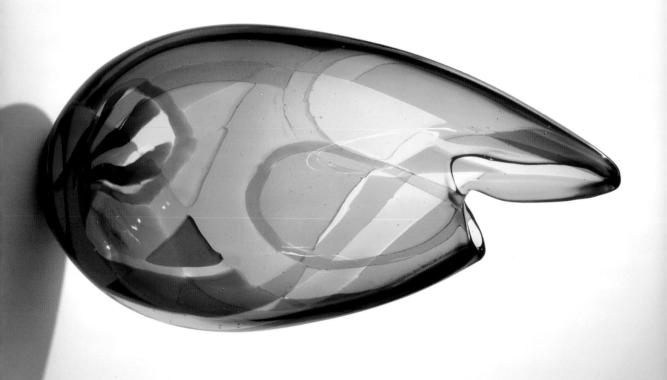

PLATE 100　**DOROTHY HAFNER**
Aurora, 1995, 18 5/8 x 9 15/16 x 6 in.
(47.31 x 25.24 x 15.20 cm)

Zanfirico

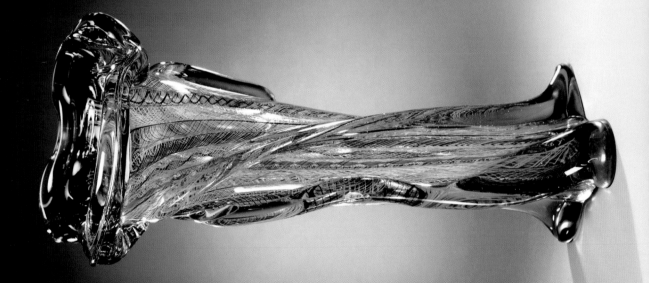

PLATE 101 **FRITZ DREISBACH**
Tall Slender Dichroic Neodymium Mongo
with Arching Serpents & Cypress Base,
1996, 22 1/4 x 11 x 11 in. (56.52 x 27.90 x 27.90 cm)

PLATE 102   **FLORA MACE AND
JOEY KIRKPATRICK**
Zanfirico Pear, 1994, 19 1/4 x diam. 12 1/4 in.
(48.90 x diam. 31.12 cm)

PLATE 103 **RICHARD MARQUIS**
Teapot Goblet, 1989, 8 1/2 x 4 1/2 x 4 1/2 in.
(21.59 x 11.43 x 11.43 cm)

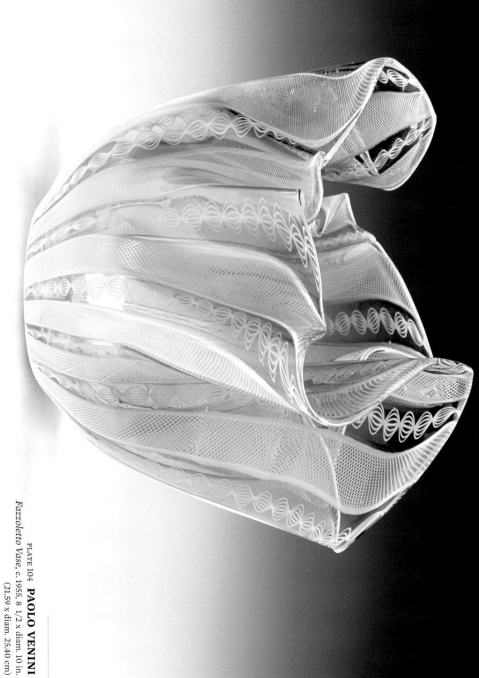

PLATE 104 **PAOLO VENINI**
Fazzoletto Vase, c. 1955, 8 1/2 x diam. 10 in.
(21.59 x diam. 25.40 cm)

Venice Today

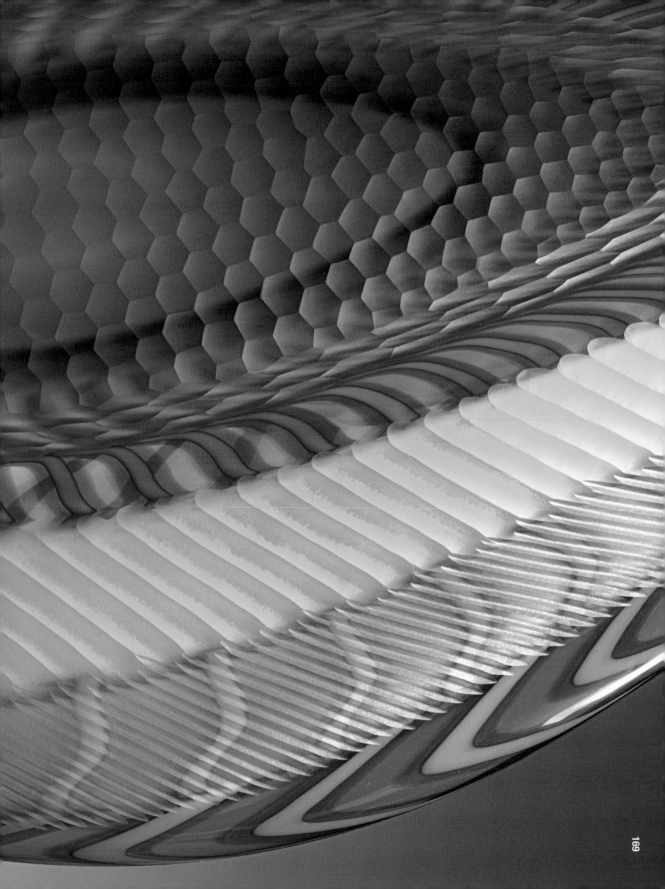

PLATE 105 **CRISTIANO BIANCHIN**
Crisaliforme, 2005–2006, 23 7/8 x diam. 3 15/16 in.
(60.64 x diam. 10 cm)

PLATE 106   **LUCIO BUBACCO**
Carnival on the Grand Canal,
1995, 15 1/4 x 21 x 21 in. (38.74 x 53.30 x 53.30 cm)

PLATE 107 **LAURA DE SANTILLANA**
Flag XVI, 2003, 15 1/2 x 16 3/4 x 2 in. (39.37 x 42.55 x 5.10 cm)

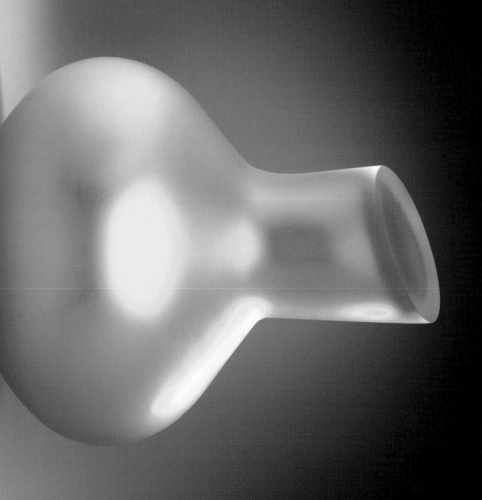

PLATE 108 **LAURA DE SANTILLANA**
Bodhi (Yellow), 2006, 17 3/4 x diam. 13 in.
(45.09 x diam. 33 cm)

PLATE 109 **MASSIMO MICHELUZZI**
Red Vase, 2003,
21 1/4 x 11 1/2 x 5 1/4 in. (53.98 x 29.21 x 13.34 cm)

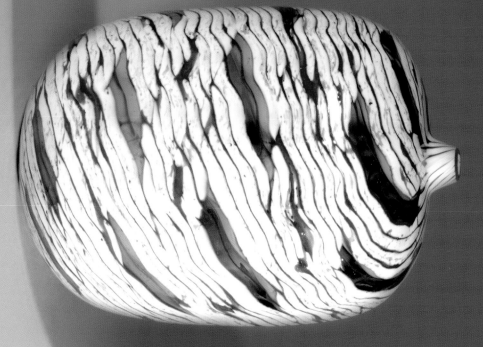

PLATE 110 **YOICHI OHIRA**
Laguna Vase, 1999,
8 3/4 x diam. 6 1/4 in. (22.23 x diam. 15.88 cm)

PLATE 111 **YOICHI OHIRA**
Murrine con Polvere Vase, 2000,
6 1/4 x 5 7/8 x 6 in. (15.88 x 14.92 x 15.24 cm)

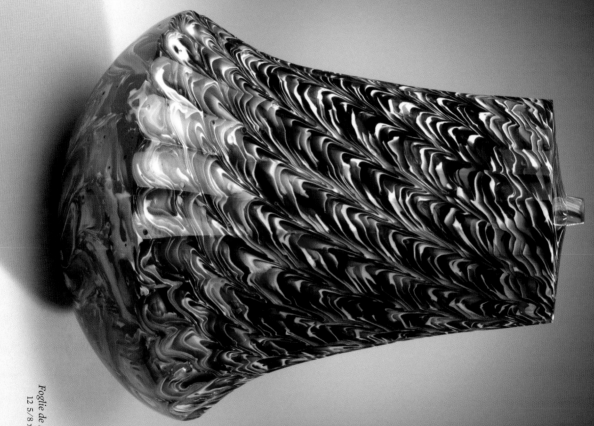

PLATE 112 **YOICHI OHIRA**
Foglie de Ninfee n. 21—Torsione: Rigadin, 2005,
12 5/8 x diam. 9 3/4 in. (32.07 x diam. 24.76 cm)

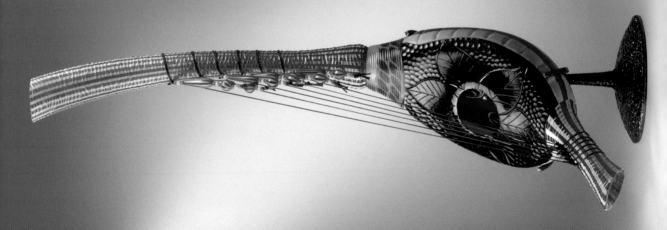

PLATE 113 **DAVIDE SALVADORE**
Spingarpa, 2006, 39 3/8 x 11 13/16 x 7 7/8 in.
(100.01 x 30 x 20 cm)

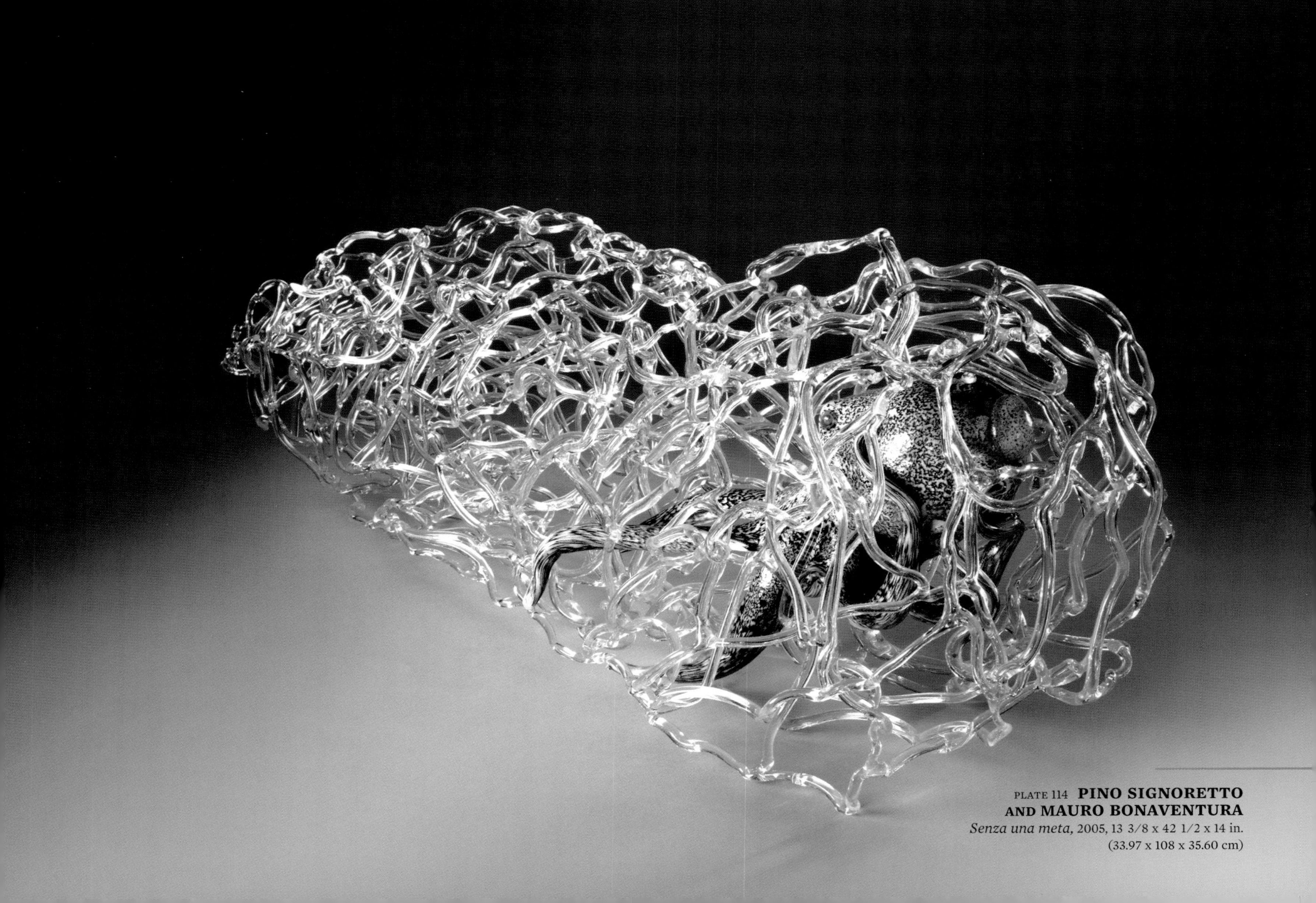

PLATE 114 **PINO SIGNORETTO
AND MAURO BONAVENTURA**
Senza una metà, 2005, 13 3/8 x 42 1/2 x 14 in.
(33.97 x 108 x 35.60 cm)

PLATE 115 **LINO TAGLIAPIETRA**
Endeavor, 1998, 42 x 128 in.
(106.68 x 325.12 cm), approximately, overall

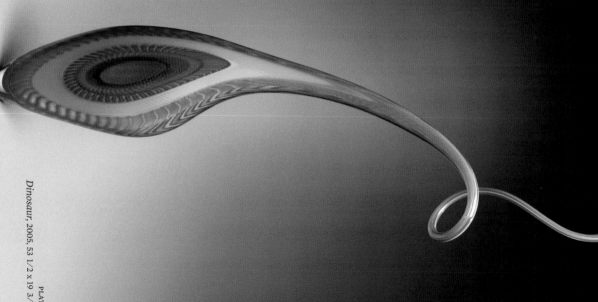

PLATE 116 **LINO TAGLIAPIETRA**
Dinosaur, 2005, 53 1/2 x 19 3/4 x 6 1/4 in. (135.89 x 50.17 x 15.88 cm)

PLATE 117 **VENINI S.p.a.**
Donna Vase and "Bolle" Bottle,
installation, Moss, 2003

Beyond Glass

PLATE 118 **FEDERICA MARANGONI**
Books of Memory, 2004, dimensions variable

PLATE 119 **FEDERICA MARANGONI**
People, 2005. 5 1/4 x 11 1/4 x 4 in. (13.34 x 28.57 x 10.20 cm)

Works in the Exhibition

Dimensions: height precedes width precedes depth

Jean Arp, designer
French, 1887–1966
with **Egidio Costantini,** director
La Fucina degli Angeli
Italian, established 1950

Nude, 1964
glass, blown and hand-formed
10 1/8 x 5 x 13 3/8 in.
(25.72 x 12.70 x 33.97 cm)
Museum of Fine Arts, Boston,
Gift of Mrs. Peggy Guggenheim

Philip Baldwin
American, b. 1947
Monica Guggisberg
Swiss, b. 1955

Blue + Red Spin, 1997
glass, blown, with *battuto*
21 1/4 x diam. 5 1/2 in.
(53.98 x diam. 13.97 cm)
Carnegie Museum of Art,
Gift of Barry Friedman Ltd., 2002.69.4

Philip Baldwin
American, b. 1947
Monica Guggisberg
Swiss, b. 1955

Faceted Plains in Red, 2001
glass, blown, with *battuto*
10 x diam. 7 7/8 in.
(25.40 x diam. 20 cm)
Carnegie Museum of Art,
Edgar L. Levenson Fund, 2001.33

Alfredo Barbini
Italian, b. 1912

Horse, 1959–1960
glass, blown, with *scavo*
10 1/4 x 23 1/2 x 4 in.
(26.04 x 59.69 x 10.20 cm)
Lent by Barry Friedman Ltd.

Alfredo Barbini
Italian, b. 1912

Biennale Vase, 1962
glass, hot-worked, with *sommerso* and *battuto*
10 x 8 1/2 x 4 1/2 in.
(25.40 x 21.60 x 11.40 cm)
The Museum of Modern Art, New York,
Gift of the Architecture and Design
Committee in honor of Ethel Shein.
Acquired with the assistance of
The Contemporary Arts Council,
Patti Cadby Birch, Jeffrey P. Klein,
Jo Carole Lauder, Brook Berlind,
Jodie Eastman, Morris Orden, Lorna
Hyde Graev, Virginia Coleman,
Sandra Lang Landsman,
Elizabeth Pozen, Judy Winslow
McBride, and Patricia Whitman, 2004

Nicolò Barovier, designer
Italian, 1886–1953
Artisti Barovier, manufacturer
Italian, established 1884

Large Vase with Inflated Murrine,
c. 1914
glass, blown, with *murrine*
18 15/16 x diam. 10 in.
(48.10 x diam. 25.40 cm)
The Corning Museum of Glass,
Corning, New York

Eugene Berman, designer
American, b. Russia, 1899–1972
Venini & C., manufacturer
Italian, 1929–1985

Obelisk with Masks, 1951
glass, hot-worked
12 13/16 x 3 1/4 x 3 3/16 in.
(32.60 x 8.20 x 8 cm)
The Corning Museum of Glass, Corning,
New York. Lent by The Steinberg
Foundation

Eugene Berman, designer
American, b. Russia, 1899–1972
Venini & C., manufacturer
Italian, 1929–1985

Vase in Form of a Well Head, 1951
glass, blown and hot-worked
5 3/4 x diam. 6 1/2 in.
(14.61 x diam. 16.51 cm)
Lent by Odetto Lastra

Cristiano Bianchin
Italian, b. 1963

Crisaliforme, 2005–2006
glass, blown; and hemp cord and elm
23 7/8 x diam. 3 15/16 in.
(60.64 x diam. 10 cm)
Carnegie Museum of Art,
Women's Committee
Acquisition Fund, 2006.54

Fulvio Bianconi, designer
Italian, 1915–1996
Venini & C., manufacturer
Italian, 1929–1985

Fazzoletto Vase, designed 1949
glass, blown
10 1/4 x diam. 11 1/2 in.
(26.04 x diam. 29.21 cm)
The Museum of Modern Art, New
York, Gift of Macy's, 1953

Fulvio Bianconi, designer
Italian, 1915–1996
Venini & C., manufacturer
Italian, 1929–1985

Pezzato Vase, 1950
glass, fused and blown, with *tesserae*
14 11/16 x 5 7/16 x 4 1/16 in.
(37.30 x 13.80 x 10.30 cm)
The Corning Museum of Glass,
Corning, New York,
Lent by The Steinberg Foundation

Fulvio Bianconi, designer
Italian, 1915–1996
Venini & C., manufacturer
Italian, 1929–1985

Fasce Orizzontali Vase, 1953–1954
glass, blown, with applied threads
12 x diam. 11 11/16 in.
(30.50 x diam. 28.10 cm)
The Corning Museum of Glass,
Corning, New York,
Lent by The Steinberg Foundation

Fulvio Bianconi, designer
Italian, 1915–1996
Venini & C., manufacturer
Italian, 1929–1985

Sasso Vase, 1966–1970
glass, blown and hot-worked
4 1/2 x 4 9/16 x 3 1/4 in.
(11.50 x 11.60 x 8.20 cm)
The Corning Museum of Glass,
Corning, New York,
Lent by The Steinberg Foundation

Fulvio Bianconi, designer
Italian, 1915–1996
Venini & C., manufacturer
Italian, 1929–1985

Sasso Vase, 1966–1970
glass, blown and hot-worked
5 3/4 x diam. 5 3/8 in.
(14.60 x diam. 13.60 cm)
The Corning Museum of Glass,
Corning, New York,
Lent by The Steinberg Foundation

Sonja Blondahl
American, b. 1952
Fuchsia/Violet, 1994
glass, blown, with *incalmo*
17 5/8 x diam. 11 5/8 in.
(44.77 x diam. 29.53 cm)
Carnegie Museum of Art,
Gift of Mr. and Mrs. William Block,
2002.51.2

Lucio Bubacco
Italian, b. 1957
Carnival on the Grand Canal, 1995
glass, flame-worked
15 1/4 x 21 x 21 in.
(38.74 x 53.30 x 53.30 cm)
Carnegie Museum of Art,
Gift of Mr. and Mrs. William Block,
2003.42.3

James Carpenter, designer
American, b. 1949
Venini & C., manufacturer
Italian, 1929–1985
Calabash, 1983
glass, blown
11 1/2 x 4 1/2 x 4 1/8 in.
(29.21 x 11.40 x 10.50 cm)
Carnegie Museum of Art, Women's
Committee Acquisition Fund, 2006.53.1

James Carpenter, designer
American, b. 1949
Venini & C., manufacturer
Italian, 1929–1985
Zebra Vase, 1985
glass, blown, with *tessuto*
7 1/2 x 4 5/16 x 7 1/16 in.
(19.10 x 11 x 17.90 cm)
Chrysler Museum of Art,
Gift of Sheri Sandler in memory
of Sam and Reba Sandler

Dale Chihuly
American, b. 1941
with **Lino Tagliapietra**, maestro
Italian, b. 1934
*Olive Green and Chrome Yellow
Venetians with Saw-Tooth Flanges*, 1988
glass, blown and hot-worked
17 3/4 x diam. 9 1/16 in.
(45.10 x diam. 23 cm)
Carnegie Museum of Art,
Gift of Mr. and Mrs. William Block,
2002.51.3

Dale Chihuly
American, b. 1941
13 1/8 x diam. 7 1/2 in.
(33.50 x diam. 19 cm)
The Corning Museum of Glass,
Corning, New York,
Gift of the artist

Dale Chihuly
American, b. 1941
*Cadmium Yellow Venetian with Red
Lilies*, 1989
glass, blown and hot-worked
19 x 14 x 16 in.
(48.30 x 35.60 x 40.60 cm)
Lent by George R. Stroemple

Dale Chihuly
American, b. 1941
Cobalt Blue Venetian #410, 1990
glass, blown and hot-worked
33 x 14 x 11 in.
(83.80 x 35.60 x 27.90 cm)
Lent by George R. Stroemple

Dale Chihuly
American, b. 1941
with **Pino Signoretto**, maestro
Italian, b. 1944
Cadmium Yellow Putti Venetian, 1993
glass, blown and hot-worked
27 x 17 x 17 in.
(68.60 x 43.20 x 43.20 cm)
Lent by George R. Stroemple

Dale Chihuly
American, b. 1941
with **Pino Signoretto**, maestro
Italian, b. 1944
*Spotted Raspberry Putti Venetian
with Devil on Sunflower*, 1994
glass, blown and hot-worked
The Corning Museum of Glass,
Corning, New York

Dale Chihuly
American, b. 1941
*Red Spotted Ikebana with Chartreuse
Stems*, 1992
glass, blown, with gold leaf
44 1/2 x 32 1/2 x 17 in.
(113.03 x 82.55 x 43.20 cm)
Lent by Dan Dailey

Dan Dailey
American, b. 1947
Venini & C., manufacturer
Italian, 1929–1985
Pistachio Lamp, 1972
glass, blown; and brass
15 1/2 x 11 x 11 in.
(39.40 x 27.90 x 27.90 cm)
Lent by Otto Piene

Dan Dailey
American, b. 1947
Venini & C., manufacturer
Italian, 1929–1985
Satturn Rocket Lamp, 1972
glass, blown; and brass
10 x 9 x 9 in.
(25.40 x 22.90 x 22.90 cm)
Carnegie Museum of Art,
Women's Committee
Acquisition Fund, 2006.37

Dan Dailey
American, b. 1947
Splendid, 2005
glass, blown, and nickel
and gold-plated brass
26 1/2 x 20 1/2 x 8 1/2 in.
(67.30 x 52.10 x 21.60 cm)
Lent by Dennis and Lois Gleicher

Dan Dailey
American, b. 1947
Numeri Plate, 1977
glass, blown and fused, with *murrine*
1 3/8 x diam. 10 3/4 in.
(3.49 x diam. 27.30 cm)
The Corning Museum of Glass,
Corning, New York

Laura de Santillana, designer
Italian, b. 1955
Venini & C., manufacturer
Italian, 1929–1985
Flag XVI, 2003
glass, blown
15 1/2 x 16 3/4 x 2 in.
(39.37 x 42.55 x 5.10 cm)
Lent by Luke and Barbara Ward

Laura de Santillana
Italian, b. 1955
Bodhi (Yellow), 2006
glass, blown and hand-ground,
with mirrored interior
17 3/4 x diam. 13 in.
(45.09 x diam. 33 cm)
Carnegie Museum of Art,
Women's Committee
Acquisition Fund, 2006.37

Nadège Desgenétez
French, b. 1973
Cages Dorées, 2004
glass, blown, with *reticello*
12 x 8 x 7 in.
(30.50 x 20.30 x 17.80 cm)
Lent by Marsha Berger and Kevin
Silson

Nadège Desgenétez
French, b. 1973
Chaussette (dark purple), 2004
glass, blown, with *incalmo*
24 1/2 x 8 3/4 x 4 1/2 in.
(62.23 x 22.22 x 11.43 cm)
Carnegie Museum of Art,
Helen Johnston Acquisition Fund,
2005.7

Fritz Dreisbach
American, b. 1941
*Tall Slender Dichroic Neodymium
Base*, 1996
Mongo with Arching Serpents & Cypress
glass, blown and hot-worked,
with *zanfirico*
22 1/4 x 11 x 11 in.
(56.52 x 27.90 x 27.90 cm)
Carnegie Museum of Art,
Gift of Mr. and Mrs. William Block,
2002.51.9

Max Ernst, designer
German, 1891–1976
with **Egidio Costantini**, director
La Fucina degli Angeli
Italian, established 1950
Bird, 1964
glass, blown and hand-formed
15 1/8 x 8 3/4 x 3 1/4 in.
(38.42 x 22.22 x 8.26 cm)
Museum of Fine Arts, Boston,
Gift of Mrs. Peggy Guggenheim

Claire Falkenstein, designer
American, 1908–1997
Salviati & C., manufacturer
Italian, established 1877

Blue and White Vase, 1972–1973
glass, blown
17 1/8 x 8 1/4 x 7 in.
(43.50 x 20.95 x 17.80 cm)

Carnegie Museum of Art,
Women's Committee Acquisition Fund,
2006.57

Claire Falkenstein, designer
American, 1908–1997
Salviati & C., manufacturer
Italian, established 1877

Bottle-Necked Vase with 2 Rings, c. 1972
glass, blown and hot-worked
9 9/16 x 6 3/16 x 3 15/16 in.
(24.30 x 15.70 x 10.10 cm)

The Corning Museum of Glass,
Corning, New York

Anzolo Fuga, designer
Italian, 1914–1998
Arte Vetraria Muranese, manufacturer
Italian, established 1932

Dish, c. 1956
glass, blown with murrine
5 x 19 x 17 in. (12.70 x 48.30 x 43.20 cm)

Carnegie Museum of Art,
Women's Committee Acquisition Fund,
2006.56

Shane Guffogg
American, b. 1962
with **Pino Signoretto**, maestro
Italian, b. 1944

Return the Find, 2005
glass, hot-worked
12 x 7 x 8 in. (30.50 x 20.30 cm)

Lent by the artist

Dorothy Hafner
American, b. 1952
with **Lino Tagliapietra**, maestro
Italian, b. 1934

Aurora, 1995
glass, blown and fused, with tesserae
18 5/8 x 9 15/16 x 6 in.
(47.31 x 25.24 x 15.20 cm)

The Corning Museum of Glass,
Corning, New York, Gift of Martin
Bresler

Paul Jenkins, designer
American, b. 1923
with **Egidio Costantini**, director
La Fucina degli Angeli
Italian, established 1950

*Phenomena One Pole of the
Twelve Pole Creek*, 1969
glass, hot-worked and hand-formed
20 1/8 x 6 1/2 x 3 1/2 in.
(51.12 x 16.51 x 8.89 cm)

Huntington Museum of Art,
Huntington, West Virginia

Paul Jenkins, designer
American, b. 1923
with **Egidio Costantini**, director
La Fucina degli Angeli
Italian, established 1950

Phenomena Blue Stele, 1970
glass, hot-worked and hand-formed
23 x 10 x 7 in.
(58.40 x 25.40 x 17.80 cm) overall
7 x 5 1/2 in. (17.80 x 13.97 cm) base

Lent by Paul and Suzanne Jenkins

Paul Jenkins, designer
American, b. 1923
with **Egidio Costantini**, director
La Fucina degli Angeli
Italian, established 1950

Phenomena Chalice Fold, 1970
glass, hot-worked and hand-formed
15 1/2 x 7 x 5 1/2 in.
(39.37 x 17.80 x 13.97 cm)

Lent by Paul and Suzanne Jenkins

Marvin Lipofsky
American, b. 1938
with **Gianni Toso**, maestro
Italian, b. 1943
made at Venini & C.
Italian, 1929–1985

Venini Series 1972 #7, 1972
glass, mold-blown, cut, and
acid-polished
8 1/2 x 12 x 10 in.
(21.59 x 30.50 x 25.40 cm)

Carnegie Museum of Art,
Women's Committee Acquisition Fund,
2005.48

Marvin Lipofsky
American, b. 1938
with **Gianni Toso**, maestro
Italian, b. 1943
made at Fratelli Toso
Italian, established 1979

Fratelli Toso Series, Split Piece,
1977–1978
glass, mold-blown, cut, and
acid-polished
7 x 13 x 10 in. (17.80 x 33 x 25.40 cm)
14 x 16 x 18 in. (35.60 x 40.60 x 45.70 cm)

Indianapolis Museum of Art,
Gift of Marilyn and Eugene Glick,
1992.147A, B

Marvin Lipofsky
American, b. 1938
with **Gianni Toso**, maestro
Italian, b. 1943
made at Fratelli Toso
Italian, established 1979

The Four Seasons—I Quattro Stagioni,
Venezia Aperto Vetro, 1998

Winter—Inverno
glass, blown, sand-blasted, and
acid-polished
17 17/1/2 x 16 1/2 in.
(43.18 x 44.45 x 41.91 cm)

Spring—Primavera
glass, blown, sand-blasted, and
acid-polished
5 x 34 x 5 in.
(12.70 x 86.36 x 12.70 cm)

Autumn—Autunno
glass, blown, sand-blasted, and
acid-polished
12 1/2 x 26 x 13 in.
(31.75 x 66.04 x 33.02 cm)

Summer—Estate
glass, mold-blown and hand-cut,
with gold leaf
12 x 18 x 14 1/2 in.
(30.48 x 45.72 x 36.83 cm)

Lent by the artist

Flora Mace
American, b. 1949
Joey Kirkpatrick
American, b. 1952

Zanfirico Pear, 1994
glass, blown, with zanfirico
19 1/4 x diam. 12 1/4 in.
(48.90 x diam. 31.12 cm)

Carnegie Museum of Art,
Gift of Mr. and Mrs. William Block,
2002.51.17

Federica Marangoni
Italian, b. 1940

Ciaobella Nikes, designed 1984
glass, hot-worked and sand-blasted
4 5/16 x 11 7/16 x 3 9/16 in.
(10.95 x 28.97 x 9.05 cm) each

Lent by the artist

Federica Marangoni
Italian, b. 1940

The Fire Dance, 1989
glass, cast; and neon and mirrored glass
8 x 34 x 43 in.
(20.30 x 86.40 x 109.20 cm)

Lent by the artist

Federica Marangoni
Italian, b. 1940

Books of Memory, 2004
glass, cast; and neon and metal
dimensions variable

Lent by Asher Remy Toledo

Federica Marangoni
Italian, b. 1940

People, 2005
glass, cast; and neon and steel
5 1/4 x 11 1/4 x 4 in.
(13.34 x 28.57 x 10.20 cm)

Lent by Asher Remy Toledo

Dante Marioni
American, b. 1964

Yellow Mosaic Vase, 1998
glass, blown, with murrine
29 1/8 x diam. 7 1/2 in.
(73.98 x diam. 19.05 cm)

Carnegie Museum of Art,
Gift of Mr. and Mrs. William Block,
2002.51.18.2

Dante Marioni
American, b. 1964
Reticello Vase, 2001
glass, blown, with reticello
26 3/4 x diam. 5 7/8 in.
(67.95 x diam. 14.92 cm)
Carnegie Museum of Art,
Gift of Mr. and Mrs. William Block,
2003.42.12

Richard Marquis
American, b. 1945
made at Venini & Co.
Italian, 1929–1985
Striped Cup, 1969
glass, blown, with cane
2 1/2 x 4 1/4 x 4 1/4 in.
(6.35 x 10.79 x 10.79 cm)
Lent by the artist

Richard Marquis
American, b. 1945
made at Venini & C.
Italian, 1929–1985
Nirmal Kaur, cloth cover
American Acid Capsule with Cloth Container, 1969–1970
glass, solid-worked with murrine, cane, and incalmo; and cloth cover
4 x diam. 1 1/4 in.
(10.20 x diam. 3.17 cm)
Lent by Pam Biallas

Richard Marquis
American, b. 1945
made at Venini & C.
Italian, 1929–1985
Nirmal Kaur, velvet cover
Stars and Stripes Cup with Container (Free Speech Cup), 1970
glass, blown, with murrine, cane, and incalmo; and velvet cover
3 1/2 x 5 1/4 x 4 in.
(8.89 x 13.34 x 10.20 cm)
Lent by Pam Biallas

Richard Marquis
American, b. 1945
made at Venini & C.
Italian, 1929–1985
Nirmal Kaur, cloth cover
Mae West Cup and Cover, 1969–1970
glass, blown, with cane; and cloth cover
3 3/16 x diam. 4 7/16 in.
(8.10 x diam. 11.25 cm)
The Corning Museum of Glass,
Corning, New York

Richard Marquis
American, b. 1945
made at Venini & C.
Italian, 1929–1985
Red Riding Hood's Grandma's House Landscape Bottle, 1970
glass, blown and hot-bit-drilled, with murrine
4 1/4 x 3 1/2 x 1 3/4 in.
(10.79 x 8.89 x 4.45 cm)
Lent by the artist

Richard Marquis
American, b. 1945
made at Venini & C.
Italian, 1929–1985
Red Riding Hood's Grandma's House Landscape Bottle, 1970
glass, blown and hot-bit-drilled, with murrine
5 1/2 x 4 3/4 x 3 in.
(13.97 x 12.07 x 7.60 cm)
Lent by Pam Biallas

Richard Marquis
American, b. 1945
made at Venini & C.
Italian, 1929–1985
Teapot Goblet, 1989
glass, blown, with zanfirico and murrine
8 1/2 x 4 1/2 x 4 1/2 in.
(21.59 x 11.43 x 11.43 cm)
Carnegie Museum of Art, Purchase:
Gift of the Henry L. Hillman Fund in
honor of Maxine and William Block,
2002.61

Richard Marquis
American, b. 1945
Marquiscarpa #19, 1991
glass, fused, slumped, blown, and wheel-carved, with murrine
5 1/4 x 7 5/16 x 4 in.
(13.34 x 18.57 x 10.16 cm)
Carnegie Museum of Art, Purchase:
Anonymous gift, by exchange, 1996.15

Dino Martens, designer
Italian, 1894–1970
Vetri Decorativi Rag. Aureliano Toso, manufacturer
Italian, 1938–1979
Bottiglia Allegria, designed 1952
glass, blown, with zanfirico
24 x diam. 4 9/16 in.
(61 x diam. 11.59 cm)
The Corning Museum of Glass,
Corning, New York, Gift of Vetreria
Artistica Rag. Aureliano Toso

Dino Martens, designer
Italian, 1894–1970
Vetri Decorativi Rag. Aureliano Toso, manufacturer
Italian, 1938–1979
Oriente Vase, 1954
glass, blown, with aventurine, zanfirico, and colored cane
15 1/2 x 7 x 4 in.
(39.37 x 17.80 x 10.20 cm)
Carnegie Museum of Art,
Women's Committee Acquisition Fund,
2006.36

Dino Martens, designer
Chrysler Museum of Art,
lent by Sheri Sandler

Napoleone Martinuzzi, designer
Italian, 1892–1977
Venini & C., manufacturer
Italian, 1929–1985
Black Cactus, 1928–1930
glass, hot-worked
13 1/2 x diam. 3 11/16 in.
(34.29 x diam. 9.37 cm)
Lent by Luke and Barbara Ward

Napoleone Martinuzzi, designer
Italian, 1892–1977
Venini & C., manufacturer
Italian, 1929–1985
Amphora, 1930
glass (pulegoso), blown
12 7/8 x 13 1/4 x 10 in.
(32.70 x 33.66 x 25.40 cm)
Lent by Barry Friedman Ltd.

Josiah McElheny
American, b. 1966
From an Historical Anecdote about Fashion, 2000
12 glass objects, blown; and display case and 5 framed digital prints
72 1/16 x 118 1/8 x 27 3/16 in.
(183.04 x 300.04 x 69.06 cm), overall
Whitney Museum of American Art,
New York; Purchase, with funds from
Wilfred P. and Rose J. Cohen Purchase
Fund and the Neysa McMein Purchase
Award; 2001.181a-cc

Josiah McElheny
American, b. 1966
The Controversy Surrounding the Veronese Vase (from the Office of Luigi Zecchin), 1996
glass, blown and metal shelving,
bulletin board, drawings, and text
shelf unit: 84 x 35 1/2 x 12 in.
(213.40 x 90.20 x 30.50 cm)
bulletin board: 25 1/4 x 37 1/4 in.
(64.10 x 94.60 cm)
Museum of Contemporary Art San
Diego, Museum purchase

Massimo Micheluzzi
Italian, b. 1957
Red Vase, 2003
glass, blown, with murrine and battuto
21 1/4 x 11 1/2 x 5 1/4 in.
(53.98 x 29.21 x 13.34 cm)
Lent by the artist

James Mongrain
American, b. 1968
Chandelier, 2007
glass, blown
dimensions undetermined at the time
of printing
Lent by the artist

Benjamin Moore
American, b. 1952
Palla Set, 1994
glass, blown
4 1/4 x diam. 18 3/4 in.
(10.79 x diam. 47.63 cm)
16 x diam. 5 in.
(40.60 x diam. 12.70 cm)
Carnegie Museum of Art,
Gift of Mr. and Mrs. William Block,
2003.42.13

Alessandro Moretti
Italian, 1922–1998

Dish in Tuning Color, 1969
glass, blown
8 3/4 x diam. 20 1/2 in.
(22.20 x diam. 52.10 cm) overall
Museum of American Glass at
Wheaton Arts and Cultural Center,
Gift of Lidia Moretti and Yvonne
Moretti

William Morris
American, b. 1957

Suspended Artifact, 1995
glass, blown, with *scavo*; and steel
stand
29 x 27 x 6 in.
(73.66 x 68.58 x 15.24 cm)
Carnegie Museum of Art,
Purchase: Anonymous gift and gift of
Mr. and Mrs. Leon A. Arkus, by
exchange, 1996.2

William Morris
American, b. 1957

Bird Rattle, 1998
glass, blown, with *scavo*
16 1/8 x 5 x 13 1/2 in.
(40.96 x 12.70 x 34.29 cm)
Lent by Luke and Barbara Ward

William Morris
American, b. 1957

Rhyton Bull, 1998
glass, blown, with *scavo*
10 1/2 x 7 3/8 x 13 1/2 in.
(26.70 x 18.70 x 34.30 cm)
Lent by Luke and Barbara Ward

Kathleen Mulcahy
American, b. 1950

In the Fire: Spinner Group in Red, 1992
glass, blown
16 x 15 1/2 x 22 in.
(40.64 x 39.37 x 55.88 cm)
26 x 5 1/4 x 9 in.
(66.04 x 13.34 x 22.86 cm)
8 1/2 x 8 x 10 in.
(21.59 x 20.32 x 25.40 cm)
3 1/2 x 3 1/4 x 8 in.
(8.89 x 8.26 x 20.32 cm)
Carnegie Museum of Art,
Mrs. James Heroy Memorial Fund and
Decorative Arts Purchase Fund,
92.34.1–4

Yoichi Ohira
Japanese, b. 1946
with **Livio Serena**, maestro
Italian, b. 1942

Laguna Vase, 1999
glass, blown, with canes and powder
8 3/4 x diam. 6 1/4 in.
(22.23 x diam. 15.88 cm)
Carnegie Museum of Art,
Harlan E. Youel Bequest Fund,
2001.16.1

Yoichi Ohira
Japanese, b. 1946
with **Livio Serena**, maestro
Italian, b. 1942

Murrine con Polvere Vase, 2000
glass, blown, with *murrine* and powder
6 1/4 x 5 7/8 x 6 in.
(15.88 x 14.92 x 15.24 cm)
Carnegie Museum of Art,
Harlan E. Youel Bequest Fund,
2001.16.2

Yoichi Ohira
Japanese, b. 1946
with **Giacomo Barbini**, maestro
Italian, b. 1951
and **Andrea Zilio**, maestro
Italian, b. 1966

Foglie de Ninfee n. 21—Torsione: Rigadin,
2005
glass, blown, with cane, *murrine*,
and powder, carved, and polished
12 5/8 x diam. 9 3/4 in.
(32.07 x diam. 24.76 cm)
Carnegie Museum of Art,
Women's Committee Acquisition Fund,
2006.55

Gio Ponti, designer
Italian, 1891–1979
Venini & C., manufacturer
Italian, 1929–1985

Bottiglie Morandiane, c. 1948–1952
glass, blown, with *incalmo*
13 x diam. 4 1/2 in.
(33 x diam. 11.43 cm)
Carnegie Museum of Art,
Ailsa Mellon Bruce Fund, 2007.13.A-B

Stephen Rolfe Powell
American, b. 1951

Acid Puffy Snoop, 2006
glass, blown, with *murrine*
28 x 23 1/2 x 20 in.
(71.10 x 59.69 x 50.80 cm)
Lent by Wallis and Marshall Katz

William Prindle
American, b. 1952
Venini & C., manufacturer
Italian, 1929–1985

Cloud Lamp, 1974
glass, mold-blown; and wood
14 x 17 x 14 in.
(35.60 x 43.20 x 35.60 cm)
Lent by the artist

Giulio Radi, designer
Italian, 1895–1952
Arte Vetraria Muranese, manufacturer
Italian, established 1932

Reazioni Policrome, c. 1947–1952
glass, blown, with *murrine*, gold, and
silver
14 1/4 x 4 1/2 x 4 1/8 in.
(36.20 x 11.43 x 10.48 cm)
Carnegie Museum of Art,
Women's Committee Acquisition Fund,
2006.53.2

Kait Rhoads
American, b. 1968

Fashion Plate, 2005
glass, blown, with cane and *murrine*
10 1/2 x 11 x 7 1/2 in.
(26.67 x 27.90 x 19.05 cm)
Carnegie Museum of Art,
Women's Committee Acquisition Fund,
2006.9

Loredano Rosin
Italian, 1936–1991

Abstract Standing Figure, c. 1970
glass, hot-worked
26 x 10 x 4 1/2 in.
(66 x 25.40 x 11.43 cm)
New Orleans Museum of Art,
Gift of Robert Willson

Loredano Rosin
Italian, 1936–1991

Two Torsos, 1979
glass, cast, with gold leaf
26 x 13 x 7 1/2 in.
(66 x 33 x 19.05 cm)
Lent by Odetto Lastra

Maria Grazia Rosin
Italian, b. 1958
with **Pino Signoretto**, maestro
Italian, b. 1944

Jelly Fish Chandelier, 2004
glass, blown; and monofilament
71 x diam. 30 in.
(180.30 x diam. 76.20 cm)
Lent by the artist and
Caterina Tognon Arte Contemporanea

Ginny Ruffner, designer
American, b. 1952
Vistosi, manufacturer
Italian, established 1945

Chandelier, 1989
glass, blown and hot-worked
39 3/4 x diam. 34 1/4 in.
(100.97 x diam. 87 cm)
The Corning Museum of Glass,
Corning, New York,
Anonymous gift

Davide Salvadore
Italian, b. 1953

Spingarpa, 2006
glass, blown, with *battuto*
39 3/8 x 11 13/16 x 7 7/8 in.
(100.01 x 30 x 20 cm)
Lent by the artist

attributed to
Salviati & C.
Italian, 1877–1995

Platter, 1890s
glass, blown, with *reticello* and *incalmo*
2 1/4 x diam. 22 in.
(5.71 x diam. 55.90 cm)
Carnegie Museum of Art,
James L. Winokur Fund, 2005.29

Emilio Santini
Italian, b. 1955
Lampadario, 2005
glass, flame-worked; and metal
76 x 60 x 60 in.
(193 x 152.40 x 152.40 cm)
Lent by the artist

Carlo Scarpa, designer
Italian, 1906–1978
Venini & C., manufacturer
Italian, 1929–1985
Battuto Vase, 1940
glass, blown, with *battuto*
7 7/8 x 6 3/4 in.
(20 x diam. 1710 cm)
The Corning Museum of Glass,
Corning, New York,
Lent by The Steinberg Foundation

Carlo Scarpa, designer
Italian, 1906–1978
Venini & C., manufacturer
Italian, 1929–1985
Battuto Vase, 1940
glass, blown, with *battuto*
10 5/16 x diam. 4 13/16 in.
(26.20 x diam. 12.20 cm)
The Corning Museum of Glass,
Corning, New York,
Lent by The Steinberg Foundation

Carlo Scarpa, designer
Italian, 1906–1978
Venini & C., manufacturer
Italian, 1929–1985
Murrine Plate, c. 1940
glass, fused and slumped, with *murrine*
2 1/4 x diam. 10 1/2 in.
(5.71 x diam. 26.67 cm)
Carnegie Museum of Art,
Women's Committee Acquisition Fund,
2005.47

Tobia Scarpa, designer
Italian, b. 1935
Venini & C., manufacturer
Italian, 1929–1985
Occhi Vase, designed 1959-1960
glass, with *murrine*
12 1/2 x 3 5/16 x 3 1/4 in.
(31.80 x 8.70 x 8.40 cm)
The Corning Museum of Glass,
Corning, New York,
Lent by The Steinberg Foundation

Kenneth George Scott, designer
American, b. Italy, 1918
Venini & C., manufacturer
Italian, 1929–1985
Three Fish and a Snail, 1950–1970
glass, solid-worked
3 x 6 1/4 in. (7.60 x 15.90 cm)
3 x 12 1/2 in. (7.60 x 31.80 cm)
2 1/2 x 5 3/4 in. (6.40 x 14.60 cm)
2 1/2 x 3 15/16 in. (10 x 6.40 cm)
Chrysler Museum of Art,
Gift of Sheri Sandler in memory
of Sam and Reba Sandler

Archimede Seguso
Italian, 1909–1999
A Merletto Vase, 1953
glass, blown, with *reticello*
9 3/4 x diam. 7 7/16 in. (24.70 x 18.90 cm)
The Corning Museum of Glass,
Corning, New York,
Lent by Martin Cohen

Archimede Seguso
Italian, 1909–1999
made at Vetreria Archimede Seguso
Italian, established 1947
Two Peasants, 1959
glass, hot-worked
11 x diam. 5 in.
(27.90 x diam. 12.70 cm)
9 3/4 x diam. 5 in.
(24.80 x diam. 12.70 cm)
Lent by Odetto Lastra

Pino Signoretto
Italian, b. 1944
Mauro Bonaventura
Italian, b. 1965

Thomas Stearns, designer
American, 1936–2006
Venini & C., manufacturer
Italian, 1929–1985
Doge Desk Lamp for Signing Decrees,
maestro
Italian, b. 1929
glass, blown, and brass-plated bronze
26 x diam. 9 in. (66 x diam. 22.90 cm)
Carnegie Museum of Art,
Women's Committee Acquisition Fund,
2004.40

Thomas Stearns, designer
American, 1936–2006
Venini & C., manufacturer
Italian, 1929–1985
Cappello del Doge, 1961–1962
glass, blown, with *incalmo*
5 3/16 x 5 7/8 x 5 1/4 in.
(13.18 x 14.92 x 13.34 cm)
The Corning Museum of Glass,
Corning, New York,
Lent by Martin Cohen

Lino Tagliapietra
Italian, b. 1934
Giano, 1992
glass, blown, with cane
13 3/4 x diam. 6 3/16 in.
(34.93 x diam. 15.72 cm)
Carnegie Museum of Art, Purchase:
Anonymous gift, by exchange, 1996.48.2

Thomas Stearns, designer
American, 1936–2006
Venini & C., manufacturer
Italian, 1929–1985
Senza una meta, 2005
glass, blown, hot-worked, and
flame-worked
13 3/8 x 42 1/2 x 14 in.
(33.97 x 108 x 35.60 cm)
The Corning Museum of Glass,
Corning, New York,
Lent by The Steinberg Foundation

Thomas Stearns, designer
American, 1936–2006
Venini & C., manufacturer
Italian, 1929–1985
with **Francesco "Checcho" Ongaro**,
maestro
c. 1961
Venini & C., manufacturer
Italian, 1929–1985
Facades of Venice, 1962
glass, blown
16 1/2 x 4 3/4 x 2 3/4 in.
(41.91 x 12.07 x 6.99 cm)
15 1/2 x 3 1/2 x 2 in.
(39.37 x 8.89 x 5.10 cm)
The Corning Museum of Glass,
Corning, New York,
Lent by The Steinberg Foundation

Lino Tagliapietra
Italian, b. 1934
Dinosaur, 2005
glass, blown, with filigree cane,
and wheel-engraved
53 1/2 x 19 3/4 x 6 1/4 in.
(135.89 x 50.17 x 15.88 cm)
Carnegie Museum of Art,
Women's Committee Acquisition Fund,
2006.24

Lino Tagliapietra
Italian, b. 1934
Borneo, 1994
glass, blown, with *zanfirico*
24 x 7 x 5 in.
(61 x 17.80 x 12.70 cm)
Carnegie Museum of Art,
Gift of Mr. and Mrs. William Block,
2003.42.21

Lino Tagliapietra
Italian, b. 1934
Endeavor, 1998
glass, blown with filigree cane,
and wheel-engraved
42 x 128 in.
(106.68 x 325.12 cm), approximately,
overall
Chrysler Museum of Art,
Purchase: acquired in honor of Harry T.
Lester and gift of Heller Gallery and
the artist

Charles Lin Tissot, designer
American, 1904–1994
Venini & C., manufacturer
Italian, 1929–1985
Chess Set, 1955
glass, blown and hot-worked, with
zanfirico
5 3/8 x 22 x 22 in.
(13.65 x 55.90 x 55.90 cm)
Lent by Charles Luke

Charles Lin Tissot, designer
American, 1904–1994
Murano manufacturer
Birdcage, 1959
glass, blown, hot-worked, and assembled with cane; and brass and plexiglass
26 3/4 x 24 x 23 1/4 in.
(67.95 x 61 x 59.05 cm)
Cooper-Hewitt National Design Museum, Smithsonian Institution, New York, Gifts of Goran F. Holmquist, 1965–1950, and Bonniers, Inc.., 1962–1968

Charles Lin Tissot, designer
American, 1904–1994
Murano manufacturer
Cypress Tree Centerpiece, 1961
glass, hot-worked; and silk
13 3/8 x diam. 20 3/4 in.
(34 x diam. 52.60 cm)
Cooper-Hewitt National Design Museum, Smithsonian Institution, New York, Gift of Mr. and Mrs. James H. Ripley, 1962

Charles Lin Tissot, designer
American, 1904–1994
Vetreria Archimede Seguso, manufacturer
Italian, 1947–1993
Faceted Candlestick, 1964
glass, blown and cold-worked
10 1/2 x diam. 4 1/2 in.
(26.67 x diam. 11.43 cm)
Lent by Paula Tissot

Gianni Toso
Italian, b. 1943
Rites of Springtime, 2006
glass, lampworked and fused
22 x 14 x 14 in.
(55.90 x 35.60 x 35.60 cm)
Lent by the artist

Charles Lin Tissot, designer
American, 1904–1994
Vetreria Archimede Seguso, manufacturer
Italian, 1947–1993
Flame Candlestick, 1964
glass, blown, hot-worked, and cut
23 1/2 x diam. 61/4 in.
(59.69 x diam. 15.88 cm)
Lent by Paula Tissot

Mark Tobey, designer
American, 1890–1976
with **Egidio Costantini**, director
La Fucina degli Angeli
Italian, established 1950
Visage, 1966
glass, cast, with applied colored-glass trailings
18 in. (45.70 cm) high
Seattle Art Museum,
Gift of Mr. and Mrs. Robert C. Warren

Mark Tobey, designer
American, 1890–1976
with **Egidio Costantini**, director
La Fucina degli Angeli,
Italian, established 1950
Volto, 1974
glass, cast, with applied colored-glass trailings
15 x 8 1/4 x 7 1/4 in.
(38.10 x 21 x 18.40 cm)
Toledo Museum of Art,
Gift of Dorothy and George Saxe

Paolo Venini, designer
Italian, 1895–1959
Venini & C., manufacturer
Italian, 1929–1985
Fazzoletto Vase, c. 1955
glass, blown, with *zanfirico*
8 1/2 x diam. 10 in.
(21.59 x diam. 25.40 cm)
Toledo Museum of Art,
Gift of Mr. and Mrs. Otto Wittmann

Venini S.p.a.
Italian, established 1986
"Bolle" Bottle, 2003
glass, blown; and metal
dimensions variable
Lent by Murray Moss and Franklin Getchell

Venini S.p.a.
Italian, established 1986
Donna Vase, 2003
glass, blown; and metal
dimensions variable
Lent by Murray Moss and Franklin Getchell

Robert Willson
American, 1912–2000
with **Loredano Rosin**, maestro
Italian, 1936–1991
and **Egidio Costantini**, director,
La Fucina degli Angeli
Italian, established 1950
Mirage Myth, 1970
glass, hot-worked
16 x 6 1/2 x 5 in.
(40.60 x 16.51 x 12.70 cm)
Lowe Art Museum, University of Miami, Gift of Mr. and Mrs. Arnold A. Saltzman

Robert Willson
American, 1912–2000
with **Pino Signoretto**, maestro
Italian, b. 1944
Texas Longhorn, c. 1983
glass, blown
16 1/4 x 11 5/8 x 5 3/4 in.
(41.28 x 29.46 x 14.61 cm)
New Orleans Museum of Art,
Gift of the artist

Robert Willson
American, 1912–2000
with **Elio Raffaeli**, maestro
Italian, b. 1936
Red Nile (People), 1991
glass, hot-worked
26 x 12 x 6 in.
(66 x 30.50 x 15.20 cm)
The Corning Museum of Glass, Corning, New York,
Gift of Margaret Pace Willson

Vittorio Zecchin
Italian, 1878–1947
V.S.M. Cappellin Venini & C.
Italian, 1921–1925
Veronese Vase, designed 1921
glass, blown
10 9/16 x diam. 5 13/16 in.
(26.83 x diam. 14.76 cm)
The Corning Museum of Glass, Corning, New York

Francesco Zecchin, designer
Italian, 1894–1986
Napoleone Martinuzzi, designer
Italian, 1892–1977
Zecchin & Martinuzzi, manufacturer
Italian, 1932–1936
Large Velato with Curly Handles, c. 1932
glass, blown
16 7/8 x 7 3/4 x 8 1/2 in.
(42.86 x 19.68 x 21.59 cm)
Lent by Barry Friedman Ltd.

Toni Zuccheri, designer
Italian, b. 1937
Venini & C., manufacturer
Italian, 1929–1985
Scolpito Vase, 1967
glass, blown, cased, and cut
13 7/16 x diam. 3 in.
(34.20 x diam. 7.75 cm)
The Corning Museum of Glass, Corning, New York,
Lent by The Steinberg Foundation

Toni Zuccheri, designer
Italian, b. 1937
Venini & C., manufacturer
Italian, 1929–1985
Tronchi Vase, 1967
glass, blown, cased, and cut
13 x diam. 2 3/4 in. (33 x diam. 7 cm)
The Corning Museum of Glass, Corning, New York,
Lent by The Steinberg Foundation

Toots Zynsky
American, b. 1951
Parapiglia, 2000
glass, threads, fused and formed
11 x 23 1/2 x 12 1/2 in. (28 x 60 x 32 cm)
Lent by Wallis and Marshall Katz

Toots Zynsky, designer
American, b. 1951
Venini & C., manufacturer
Italian, 1929–1985
Chiacchiera, 1984
glass, blown with trailed threads
10 1/2 x diam. 7 in.
(26.67 x diam. 17.80 cm)
13 x diam. 7 in. (33 x diam. 17.80 cm)
Lent by Joe and Molly Walton

Lenders to the Exhibition

Barry Friedman Ltd.

Marsha Berger and Kevin Silson

Pam Biallas

Caterina Tognon Arte Contemporanea

Chrysler Museum of Art, Norfolk, Virginia

Martin Cohen

Cooper-Hewitt National Design Museum,
Smithsonian Institution, New York

The Corning Museum of Glass, Corning, New York

Dan Dailey

Galleria Vetro & Arte

Dennis and Lois Gleicher

Shane Guffogg

Huntington Museum of Art, Huntington, West Virginia

Indianapolis Museum of Art

Paul and Suzanne Jenkins

Wallis and Marshall Katz

Odetto Lastra

Marvin Lipofsky

Lowe Art Museum, University of Miami, Florida

Charles Luke

Federica Marangoni

Richard Marquis

James Mongrain

Murray Moss and Franklin Getchell

Museum of American Glass, Wheaton Arts
and Cultural Center, Millville, New Jersey

Museum of Contemporary Art San Diego

Museum of Fine Arts, Boston

The Museum of Modern Art, New York

New Orleans Museum of Art

Otto Piene

William Prindle

Maria Grazia Rosin

Davide Salvadore

Emilio Santini

Seattle Art Museum

The Steinberg Foundation

George R. Stroemple

Paula Tissot

Asher Remy Toledo

Toledo Museum of Art

Gianni Toso

Joe and Molly Walton

Luke and Barbara Ward

Whitney Museum of American Art, New York

Curator's Acknowledgments

This publication and exhibition were accomplished with the participation of many dedicated individuals both inside and outside the museum.

I wish particularly to acknowledge "Pittsburgh Celebrates Glass," a regional initiative to focus attention on the city and its historical connection to glass manufacturing and design, for making *Viva Vetro! Glass Alive! Venice and America* a centerpiece of its programming. The exhibition would not have come to fruition without the support and encouragement of Richard Armstrong, The Henry J. Heinz II Director of Carnegie Museum of Art, and his enthusiasm for "Pittsburgh Celebrates Glass." I also thank Marcia Gumberg, past chair, and Bill Hunt, current chair, as well as all of the members of the Museum of Art's Board, who have demonstrated unfailing commitment to this project through their endorsement of the museum's many glass acquisitions for this exhibition. The Women's Committee, led by former and current presidents Gail Murphy and Ranny Ferguson, respectively, also has been a generous and active supporter through acquisition funds for glass objects.

My sincere thanks to all the people who have worked on this publication. Arlene Sanderson, head of publications, has expertly and with great energy, intelligence, and determination shepherded this publication through every stage; Brooke Sansosti; rights and reproductions

coordinator, researched and tracked all of the images with great persistence. I am grateful to essayists Susanne Frantz and Matthew Kangas for their substantial contributions to this publication, as well as to Peter Harholdt for his superlative photography and to Tom Little. My sincere thanks to Melinda Harkiewicz, publications associate, Michelle Piranio, editor, and Polly Koch, proofreader, for their participation in this catalogue.

We are indebted to the private collectors, museums, artists, and dealers who have generously lent objects to the exhibition. Their names appear in the list of lenders. I am also extremely appreciative of the generosity of Maxine and the late William Block. Their gifts to the collection galvanized the museum's interest in contemporary glass, and several are included in this exhibition. Additionally, I wish to thank Gary Baker, Jenine Culligan, Carole Hochman, Tina Oldknow, Caterina Tognon, Asher Remy Toledo, and Verena Wasmuth, who facilitated loans to this exhibition.

This project entailed traveling in the United States and Venice, visiting artists and their descendants, collectors, dealers, museums, libraries, and scholars who graciously gave of their time, expertise, and frequently their hospitality. I thank Mitchell Algus, Louisa Bann, and the staff at the Tiffany & Co. Archives; Marina Barovier; Cristiano Bianchin; Sara Blumberg and Jim Oliveira; Domenico Cavallaro; Sarah Coffin; Martin Cohen; Dan Dailey; Barry

Friedman; Douglas Heller; Beth Hylen, Gail Bardan and the staff of the Rakow Research Library; Matthew Kangas; Odetto Lastra; Jennifer Lewis; Marvin Lipofsky; Howard J. Lockwood; Federica Marangoni; Rosa Barovier Mentasti; James Mongrain; Benjamin Moore; Yvonne Moretti; Murray Moss; Tina Oldknow; Kait Rhoads; Dino Rosin; Maria Grazia Rosin; Davide Salvadore; Alvise Schiavon; Livio Seguso; Harold Stevenson; Paula Tissot; and Caterina Tognon.

I wish to acknowledge my curatorial colleagues at Carnegie Museum of Art for their interest and support. I am indebted to Lulu Lippincott, chief curator, for her support and contributions to this exhibition and catalogue. I am particularly appreciative of the enthusiastic and relentless work and attention to detail that Rachel Delphia, assistant curator of decorative arts, and Lucy Stewart, assistant curator of education, have brought to the project. They have been the glue that has held the project together. I thank the entire museum staff for their tireless efforts to make this exhibition and its related programs and publication a reality. Special thanks to Anne Mundell for her sensitive exhibition design and to graphic designer Dale McNutt for his exciting vision for the exhibition and catalogue.

SARAH NICHOLS
Curator

195

Reproduction Credits

Index of Artists, Maestros, and Manufacturers

Susanne K. Frantz is an art historian and a former curator of 20th-century glass at the Corning Museum of Glass. She held that position for 13 years until relocating to the Czech Republic in 1998 as a Fulbright Research Scholar. In 1985, while a curator at the Tucson Museum of Art, she organized *Sculptural Glass*, the first American exhibition of site-specific installations using the medium of glass. Frantz's book, *Contemporary Glass: A World Survey from The Corning Museum of Glass* (1989), remains a primary reference in the field. In 1996, she was awarded the Henry Allen Moe Prize for writing of distinction in the arts. Frantz is a member of the International Council of the Pilchuck Glass School, former president of the Glass Art Society, and an honorary life member of that organization. She also edits the *Glass Art Society Journal*.

Matthew Kangas is an author and art critic. His book *Robert Willson: Image-Maker* on the Texas glass artist who first went to Murano was a 2002 finalist for the Washington State Book Awards. He has been a Renwick Fellow in American Crafts at the Smithsonian American Art Museum and has been awarded the Everson Medal, a National Endowment for the Arts Visual Arts Critics Fellowship. He is a corresponding editor at *Art in America* and a contributing editor for *Sculpture* and *GLASS*. He lectures widely in the United States and at major conferences around the world. Kangas received his B.A. in literature from Reed College and his M.A. in English literature from Oxford University, The Queen's College. He lives and works in Seattle, Washington.

Viva Vetro! Glass Alive! Venice and America

Arlene Sanderson, Head of Publications

Melinda Harkiewicz, Publications Associate

Brooke Sansosti, Coordinator of Rights and Reproductions

EDITOR:	Michelle Piranio
PROOFREADER:	Polly Koch
DESIGN:	Soho Invention
DIGITAL SPECIALIST:	David Bernhardt
PRINTING:	J. B. Kreider, Pittsburgh
TYPEFACES:	Mercury and Whitney by Hoefler & Frere Jones, New York
PAPER:	McCoy Silk

LIBRARY OF CONGRESS CATALOGING-IN-PUBLICATION DATA

Frantz, Susanne K.

Viva vetro! = Glass alive! : Venice and America / essays by Susanne Frantz, Matthew Kangas.

p. cm.

Catalog of an exhibition at the Carnegie Museum of Art, May 2–Sept. 16, 2007.

ISBN 978-0-88039-048-4

1. Glass art--United States--History--21st century--Exhibitions. 2. Glass art--United States--Italian influences. 3. Glass art--Italy--Murano--History--21st century--Exhibitions. 4. Glass art--Italy--Murano--American influences--Exhibitions. I. Kangas, Matthew. II. Carnegie Museum of Art. III. Title. IV. Title: Venice and America. V. Title: Glass alive.

NK5112.F68 2007

748.0945'31o973--dc22

2007014444

Carnegie Museum of Art, 4400 Forbes Avenue, Pittsburgh, Pennsylvania 15213-4080
www.cmoa.org